Simply Bob

Other books by Robert Brown

Personal Wisdom

Things I Learned From My Wife

Transparent Management

Earn Their Loyalty

Mistake-Proofing Leadership (with Rudy F. Williams)

The People Side of Lean Thinking

The HST Model for Change

The Dark Matter and Dark Energy of Lean Thinking

New Darwinian Laws Every Business Should Know (with Pat Edmonds)

Invivo (a novel)

Kids Character Building Tool Kit

Mayhem at the Open (a novel)

Murder on the Tour (a novel)

The Way of Golf

The Golfing Mind

The Golf Gods

Simply Bob

Searching for the Essence

Robert Brown

Denro Classics

Requests for permission to use or reproduce material from this book
should be directed to books@collwisdom.com

Some names have been changed to protect privacy

Former titles: Life Is Not Enough,
To Touch and Be Touched

Cover by Elm Street Design
Front cover photo:
Meryl Schenker, Seattle WA
Back cover, unknown, Ann Arbor, MI

Published by Denro Classics
11700 Mukilteo Speedway #201-1084
Mukilteo WA 98275
USA

Printed in the United States of America
by Create Space

Paper
ISBN-13: 978-0-9836768-6-7
ISBN-10: 0-9836768-6-0

Hardback
ISBN-13: 978-09836768-8-1
ISBN-10: 0-9836768-8-7

To my teachers—which means
just about everyone

The mass of men lead lives of quiet desperation and go to the grave with the song still in them.

Henry David Thoreau

~ The Beginning ~

On May twenty-first, 1946, at Mercy Hospital in Ann Arbor, Michigan, at a decent hour and with dispatch, I entered the scene. I knew right from the start that I was okay; it was the rest of the world that worried me.

World War II had just ended. In fact, President Harry Truman didn't officially declare the end of the war until I was seven months old. Other events of this auspicious time included: Emperor Hirohito of Japan declared that he wasn't a god; people paid ten cents for a loaf of bread while the minimum wage was forty cents an hour; the US military was racially segregated; and one of the best songs on the Hit Parade was "The Gypsy" by the Ink Spots.

Growing up in the middle of it all was me, asking questions and looking for answers. I wanted to use my turn wisely yet in the background my personal clock was already ticking. How best to live my allotted days? Does life, especially human life, have an essence, some quality that makes it special? Is the meaning of life personal or is it the same for everyone? This is my account of what I eventually figured out.

Famous people have biographers to tell their stories. Others—those with free time, a tale to share and a way with words—compose an autobiography or memoir. A memoir by an unknown like me suggests either an inflated ego or a genuine belief that I have something important to share. Unfortunately, a flotilla of others has similar beliefs. Neil Genzlinger, in a *New York Times* article three or four years ago, "The Problem With Memoirs," complained:

> Memoirs have been disgorged by virtually everyone who has ever had cancer, been anorexic, battled depression, lost weight. By anyone who has ever taught an underprivileged child, adopted an underprivileged child or been an underprivileged child. By anyone who was raised in the '60s, '70s or '80s, not to mention the '50s, '40s or '30s. Owned a dog. Run a marathon. Found religion. Held a job.

I wrote this memoir because of two realizations: 1) I learned that anyone can be your teacher, which means I may have something of value for you and 2) my ordinary life turned out more profound than I had any right to expect. Given my modest talents I have lived an extraordinary life. I am content and wish that for everyone.

Realization number one occurred when I was a psychology graduate student in 1969 studying the complexities of human existence at the same time I was in the navy defending our country against communism. While on duty I brought coffee to the officers, wiped their spills off counters and mopped them off floors, emptied ashtrays and, for my official job, copied coded numbers and letters from rough notes onto a clean twelve-by-twenty sheet of paper. I know, not exactly an inspiring defense of American freedoms. During school, however, I conversed with giants and pondered the great issues of humankind. At that time, I was examining the existential question of who is more involved in life, a participant in the thick of things or an observer who can see the big picture.

In the shadowy depths of an empty hangar one afternoon, I sat with a fellow sailor on low stacks of airplane tires waiting for our squadron of fighter jets to return. To make things more understandable for someone who wasn't able to finish high school, I explained my participant-observer dilemma through the metaphor of a basketball game, being either a player or spectator. "Which is a better way to be involved in the game?" I asked my simple friend, expecting him to shrug and say, "I don't know." Instead he answered, "It's whatever you want." I was silent for a moment, completely taken aback. Of course it's whatever you want. Why didn't I see that? In that moment—two guys sitting on airplane tires discussing life—this slight, not very bright young sailor in faded dungarees was my teacher. In the same way my sailor friend enlightened me, I hope to provide something of value for you.

I want to share my search for the meaning of life. What I have written is, to the best of my recollection, true. However, accuracy is not important. A friend of mine once commented on his religion, "It doesn't have to be verifiably true," he said about their dogma, "it just has to be right." In that same spirit, what I've written is as right as I can make it. This memoir describes my search and includes a few extra thoughts in the Detritus section and a few sources of inspiration and influence in the section after that.

I define myself as slightly above average, with a few highs and not too many lows. I can't spell, remember names, faces or phone numbers, or much of anything else, and my mechanical aptitude was officially measured in the fifth percentile (which means most household repairs hold the potential for disaster). I was a mediocre scholar, tight with a penny and maybe three times a year I behave like a complete jerk.

On the plus side, I'm a fair to good athlete, am compassionate, hardworking and willing to admit mistakes. As for intelligence, I'd be welcomed at a Mensa meeting, but my mental firepower is tempered by a severe case of naivety, maybe even outright gullibility. I'm good in the present, pretty much forget the past, and don't do well understanding the nuances of the future. I'd make a terrible strategist in just about everything.

However, on most measures of ability and other definable human characteristics, I'm above average. I don't think I'm great in anything, but I'm below average in only a few relatively unimportant areas. Letter grade-wise, I rate myself an uninflated B.

Although in the larger world I'm above average, in my family I am not. My four-year-old granddaughter declared confidently that my poor memory was because I "have the smallest brain in the family." I believe she is right. My brain is shrinking more each day and now is the time to tell my story before it is too late and my brain disappears altogether.

Which brings us to the issue of my story being of benefit to you. What good is reading the memoir of an above-average guy who is below average in his own family? Memoirs should be written by interesting people about interesting things or according to Neil Genzlinger, not written at all. I'm not very interesting, while over the past three thousand years or so very famous and very wise men and women have already written about the big questions of human existence. What is different here is that the insights I have gained allowed this slightly above-average person to live an extraordinary life. The New York Yankees Hall of Fame catcher Yogi Berra once said, "If you come to a fork in the road, take it." That's pretty much what I have been able to do, many times.

For me (and everyone else), the main challenge of life has been to finally understand who I am, to accept who I am and to express what that is. I am and will be the only one of me. I think that's a big deal. An additional challenge is how to be this unique person given all the pressures and influences of life, and to be the best me, however that can be done. I was lucky; I had excellent teachers, some famous, with whom I could sit down over coffee and learn from. I've had the right friends who were willing to share difficult truths. Even those who didn't like me seemed eager to share their particular insights for my personal improvement. I listened to all of them. I also tried out much of what they suggested and learned from my successes and failures.

This book is the backstory for my earlier book *Personal Wisdom* which, between the first inklings of the concept and eventual publication, took almost twenty-five years of pondering, discussing and writing. In that book I was concerned about how traditions can keep people rooted in the past and how current fads can push people in wrong directions. I advocated for people to stop being rule followers and become rule makers. I also shared a little of how I acquired personal wisdom; this is the more complete story.

This book acknowledges the finality of death and emphasizes the responsibilities of life. I've lost family and friends and know my turn is coming much too soon. I can imagine lying in a hospital bed thinking that I've pictured this moment for years and now it's arrived. It's an unsettling thought. In that future hospital bed I want to feel the contentment of a life well lived and not regret missed opportunities, the transient rewards of selfishness, a wasted life.

In 1946 the world had some growing up to do and, of course, so did I.

CONTENTS

THE MEMOIR

~ My First Great Year ~

I was seventeen. I had a good year when I was fourteen and discovered what girls were all about, but that
didn't last so I couldn't consider it a great year, especially
since my parents refused my pleas to buy a Lambretta
motor scooter. Kenny Cox from across the street had
one. I can still see him peeling out his driveway in a steep
lean and racing down the street. And I can still hear the
whine of the engine and the clicks as he shifted gears. Of
course, I didn't have the money to actually buy a scooter,
or pay for insurance and gas, and there was no place to
park it, but I really, really wanted one.

For the record, this was the kind of year the world was
having: first-class postage went from four to five cents;
ZIP codes were introduced; the Beatles were gaining
fame in Europe; Governor of Alabama George Wallace's
inauguration address included these six uplifting words,
"Segregation now, segregation tomorrow, segregation
forever"; radio stations labeled "Louie, Louie" obscene;
and the thirty-fifth president of the United States, John
F. Kennedy, was assassinated in Dallas, Texas.

In 1963, I was just beginning to dream and the vision of
Camelot was dead.

I won a tennis varsity letter for being half of the number one doubles team. This allowed me to wear a white letter sweater to school every Friday. It also meant pulling on a leather and felt varsity jacket no matter how hot the morning. I was a jock—junior grade, because it was tennis, not football, basketball or baseball. The redeeming feature was that some tennis players played these sports, which I hoped would give tennis a little cachet. It didn't, of course, but I was good at tennis and not good at anything else. A varsity letter was worth the stigma.

In my school, taking college prep courses made me one of the early nerds. Some of my neighborhood friends were hoods, looking cool in black slacks and white T-shirts with a pack of cigarettes tucked into one rolled-up sleeve and, most potently, black shoes with pointed toes as sharp as a knife. My mother wouldn't allow me to wear those points, but finally approved a pair of black Flagg Flyers with an external tongue that flipped up and down to open and close the shoe. At the same time, I was enamored of folk music, sad ballads and the self-image of being a deep-thinking beatnik, which I became simply by wearing a dark turtleneck sweater and blue jeans. I dressed any style well enough to be a qualified middle-of-the-pack member of every school and neighborhood clique, no matter how large, small or antisocial.

My life at seventeen was about as satisfying as anyone could ask for. In the early sixties it was good to be male, white, decently smart and living in the suburbs of Detroit. I kept out of trouble and adults seemed to think I was a good kid. Teachers were kind and supportive. I was personable, an odd trait in a teenager. Life was unfolding well.

Here's how my high school life could be. My biology lab mate, Eddie (as we shall call him, after smarmy Eddie Haskell of TV's *Leave It to Beaver* sitcom fame), kept bragging about how superior his lab reports were.

"Hi Bob," he said one morning. "We got our lab reports back and I got another hundred. You," he added, pointing to my report sitting on the top of the lab desk, "got an eighty-six, not bad, a solid B."

"Thanks," I said, picking up my report and looking inside, which confirmed what he said.

"This is my fifth hundred in a row. I don't think I've gotten anything less than ninety or a ninety-one. My average has to be a ninety-seven or ninety-eight, at least. Have you gotten anything above a ninety yet?"

"Not yet."

"We should get our national test results today. I'm really looking forward to finding out how well we did."

As he said that, our teacher walked into the room and announced that he indeed had our national science achievement test scores. He said we'd all done pretty well and he would hand out the scores later, but there was one surprise he wanted to share. At that point, Eddie was shaking with excitement. This was the news he was waiting for. One student, the teacher said, had done extremely well.

He looked straight at Eddie and said, "Eddie, eighty-seventh percentile nationally, that's quite an achievement." Eddie beamed, and looked at me with an expression I can only describe as saying, "I am Mr. Genius (and you're not)."

The teacher continued. "But that was not the surprise." He paused for dramatic effect. "One of our class scored at the ninety-sixth percentile." He looked at me. "Bob, well done."

I was proud of my humble acceptance of the teacher's praise, my wry smile toward my fellow students, and my gentle wave to acknowledge the thunderous applause that echoed off the lab walls. I declined being carried down the hallway on the shoulders of my classmates. Never, ever have I been more satisfied with such a karmic outcome. Victory was sweet, but it was a bit sad, too. Comeuppance is a tough experience, especially for someone like Eddie. I didn't know my own devil's handshake was only a few weeks away. Got an A in the class, although up to that point I had been grazing in the land of B.

I took our Swedish exchange student to our junior prom. My invitation and our subsequent date were written up in our local paper and included a quarter-page photo. I had heard that Swedish movies included bare breasts and simulated sex. Made me wonder what our exchange student might be interested in doing. As senior class vice president elect, I was pressured into making sure she had a date, and the date had to be an acceptable example of our school and American culture. I was promoted as the perfect representative of gentlemanly conduct. She was a beautiful blonde with a movie-star figure, so I was happy to ask her and happy when she accepted. She turned out to be a door hanger, didn't like dancing, didn't really enjoy the culture of the Motor City and didn't really like me. Not even a kiss at the door when I took her home. I ended up fulfilling a civic duty and still living midcentury, middle-class American morals.

My social highlight of the year occurred at one of our basketball games. I spotted a girl I had never seen before in the crowd. She was beautiful—her hair, her figure, her smile; I was gob-smacked. Didn't know it could happen, but it happened to me. We became high school and college sweethearts. I married her right after we graduated from college.

So far, so good. Age seventeen was about as easy and satisfying as it could have been. One moment, however, lasting all of six or seven seconds, took my life down a path I could not have imagined. My emerging worldview and sense of well-being were eviscerated; I took a hit I don't think will ever heal.

This event had its genesis maybe ten years earlier when I discovered my dad's small collection of history books, including a two-volume set, *World War II in Pictures*. With horrified fascination I returned again and again to peer at the photos of double rows of hangings, men slumped at posts after executions and worst, men standing in line, arms tied behind their backs, waiting to roll down a slope to be bayoneted by Japanese soldiers. I had seen photos in magazines of southern blacks with twisted necks hanging from trees so the brutality of death wasn't new, but the World War II photos were incomprehensible. This was horror on such a colossal scale it didn't make sense. But that was transient distress; my life at seventeen was filled with the concerns of a teenage male: getting the family car on Saturday night, wishing my face would clear up, camouflaging inconvenient erections and otherwise trying to look cool.

My world changed one afternoon in a social studies course called Intercultural Relations, an advanced class for college prep students. We were studying World War II. The teacher put on a scratchy black and white documentary movie and left the room, headed to the teachers' lounge for a smoke. We watched the usual bombs falling out of planes, big guns lobbing shells into cities and sides of buildings burning and crashing down into piles of smoky rubble.

Then the scene changed, becoming more intimate and darker. An American pilot was on his knees between two sets of railroad tracks in an industrial area. His head was down. No one else was visible. A Japanese soldier entered from offscreen with a rifle, pointed it at the pilot's head and pulled the trigger. The pilot slumped to the ground. The soldier walked away. The movie moved on to other portrayals of the war.

I was stunned. I had never witnessed someone actually being killed before. The casualness was horrifying. There was no ceremony like in the movies or on TV. No roll of drums. No blindfold. No final cigarette. The event was as casual as going to the store and buying a loaf of bread. The pilot was alive and then was dead, lying between ordinary railroad tracks outside a factory on a cold, gray day. The soldier who shot him and then walked away could have returned to a delayed breakfast or maybe to a place nearby to shoot someone else, it didn't matter.

The bell rang and we all gathered our books, three-ring binders, pencils and pens and rambled into the hall to join hundreds of other students.

The image of the pilot and the soldier haunted me down the hallway and to my locker. Other students jostled one another, slammed locker doors, yelled down the hallway, but I heard nothing; only the silence of the pilot lying still and the soldier walking away.

How was I supposed to comprehend this? My only field of battle was a tennis court. It wasn't even a tough sport like football. In football you smash into people and they smash into you. You try to knock them down and they try to knock you down. You get bruised; maybe there is blood. Excitement multiplies every second, people in the stands are cheering, standing up as the player runs to daylight, and groaning and sitting when he's tackled. If you were a player, the next day you're tired, sore, you can see the black and yellow of your wounds. Football is ceremonial mayhem, the surest and finest road to high school glory.

In tennis we wore tight white shorts, tight white shirts, white socks and white shoes. As gentlemen tennis players, we kept our own score and called our own lines, the ball out or in. One time I hit an overhead smash, really pounded the ball and the other boy called it out. Coach was watching; I was open-mouthed at the call. He had made it clear that he didn't want any of us wildly smashing at our overhead shots, something we teenage boys did regularly. Coach came over and said, "He really needed to see the ball as out. You keep playing well, and make the correct calls." He wasn't mad. I was worried because he'd said that anyone he saw missing an overhead would have to run laps. That was my only concern about the out call, running laps.

Tennis is genteel. If you're uncertain if the ball is out or in, you make the call to the benefit of your opponent. That's what we were taught and what all of us on our team did. It was actually fun. Our shot might have hit close to the line and our opponent had to call it good or out. Sometimes they'd admit, "Didn't see it," and we would have to call it. Saying "It was out" about our own shot felt good. Opponents often caught on to calling close ones in the other's favor and we would have a grand match. Some of the other teams didn't play that way, which gave us added incentive to beat them. Fair was its own reward and dishonesty was a call to action.

Now a man was dead. Twenty years earlier, half a world away, this killing had actually happened. A man, maybe a father, a brother, a husband, certainly a son, was forced to kneel down on the stones between railroad tracks and was deliberately shot in the back of the head. Someone had ordered that this man should die. Others probably watched. A few had to pick up the body and do something with it. A photographer stood to the side to take pictures. This piece of film was intentionally spliced into others to make a documentary that a producer had decided was ready to be seen. Thousands have looked at it. Why me? Why did I have to see it?

I talked to the other kids in the class. Their only concern was which parts of the movie might be on the test.

I felt the absence that was left by the killing. A man wasn't coming home. No children would be born; any children he had wouldn't see their father anymore; his wife became a widow. His parents could change the blue star in the front window of their home to gold. Maybe they did; it must have been with a heartbreakingly hollow sense of sacrifice.

My paternal grandfather died in World War I, a victim of mustard gas in the trenches. My maternal grandfather died of a heart attack, collapsing on a street in Glasgow, Scotland, years before I was born. My only uncle on my mother's side died in London during an air raid in World War II. When I was a child both my grandmothers were still alive and living in Scotland, along with my father's surviving siblings and half-siblings, maybe eight in all. In my lifetime, death hadn't visited my family and family wasn't nearby anyway.

I had no place to put the image of the killing. I had no understanding of what legitimized shooting someone in the back of the head. I had no idea about life beyond my white, middle-class, suburban boundaries.

I didn't sleep much for a week, didn't study or go out either. This began the era when my mother noted, "He never smiled." I wasn't sad; I don't think I was even depressed. I was more disappointed that life was so barbaric and man's inhumanity to man so normal.

Before the movie, I was under the impression that I was growing up in a world that made sense; that leaders knew the right things to do and did whatever that was. I accepted that a few bad people did bad things, but believed that many smart people, smarter and more experienced than I, made smart decisions and the world continually matured. That didn't seem to be the case. The world man was creating was far from the civilized place I thought it was. But I was a kid; who was I to complain? The world just was and maybe growing up was to accept that.

What made 1963 my first great year was the recognition that I knew nothing of importance. I began the quest to figure out life—where it goes and what to do with it. I could no longer trust that those in charge had some invisible store of wisdom and were taking good care of the world. It seemed that doing the right thing was up to me and I had to figure out what that was. What is the essence of being alive—of being human?

At the same time, my religious faith was faltering under the onslaught of science and boredom. Stories of God sounded more and more like fairy tales. He was either unconcerned or was losing the struggle with the Devil. Everything I had trusted and counted on until that time I found severely wanting.

It wasn't supposed to be like this.

~ God ~

A robust discussion of the meaning of life must begin at the beginning, the absolute beginning—the origin of the universe, life and humankind—and must include the future of these things. For many people, all this is in the hands of God. Until I was twenty, my concept of God, heaven and earth was what I had learned in Sunday school, which I attended until I was about twelve. My parents were believers, but not attendees. My older sister attended regular church services at our local Free Methodist church with her friend from across the street. My younger brother and I walked to Sunday school together until I realized we didn't have to actually go to the church and could instead play in the park and spend our collection money on candy. Neither my parents nor God ever seemed to learn of this sacrilege.

Until I was twenty, I believed in Adam and Eve, Moses, the Devil, God, Jesus, and had a degree of understanding of the Holy Ghost and concepts like original sin. At twenty, my college roommate John, who had been educated in a seminary, was studying ancient languages in order to read holy books in their original form and told me only an idiot believed the ancient stories. He said

Bible stories were just that, stories—stories to make a point, not define the truth.

That made everything much more difficult. My initial beliefs had enabled me to accept God without reservation as the one absolute truth in the universe. Now I learned that God was as fictionalized as the Jolly Green Giant and Superman.

John was quintessentially religious with God and toward his studies. No matter what time of day or day of the week I came home, he would be at his desk, face deep in a book. If not at his desk, he was at class, church services or the library, his face in a book there too. Pious. I learned what pious was and that I wasn't. I was drinking, hanging out at my girlfriend's apartment, staying up late and rarely making it to eight o'clock classes.

Then John met Susan. Instead of seeing him at his desk, now I saw only an empty desk until John arrived late at night or even the next morning, to report that he and his lady friend had spent hours at the park looking at the stars and the planets... yeah, of course you did, and I was Hammurabi. Maybe religion was not quite the total commitment I thought it was. Piety so easily lost to a pretty face. Or was this the Devil's work? Maybe it was a lesson for me, a lapsed believer, sent down from God through John. Was this a sign? Or was it a young guy doing what a young guy's gotta do and not about me at all? How are you supposed to identify such celestial signals?

It was easy when God was in heaven, the Devil was in hell and they were battling for my soul. But if the stories of Adam and Eve, Moses, and Noah were only stories, what else was fiction rather than truth? Were the stories of Christianity any truer than the stories of Hinduism? Did I believe only because these were the stories I grew up hearing? And if John was wrong and the stories were true, there were still the equally plausible stories of other religions, many having seniority over Christianity.

At seventeen I began to question the meaning of life. At twenty I began wondering about God and everlasting life. My investigative guide into the mysteries of eternity was a statement by Lenny Bruce, "Never trust a preacher with more than two suits." What religion wasn't self-serving, better than the alternatives, advertising that this was the one and only way to salvation? And what was with salvation? If Adam and Eve in the Garden of Eden was only a story, where did original sin come from? Did God design it in as part of our birthright? The Devil, as I understand it, was invented by Jews about the seventh century BCE to soften what had become a bipolar God responsible for both good and evil. The new fallen angel with increasing power took the heat off the good Guy and we could worship a positive heavenly image. Or is this a story too, made up by the Devil or maybe by an imaginative prophet hunched over a tablet in a mud hut? What is truth and what is spin? More and more, as I moved through my twenties, it seemed all spin to me.

My friend J. Corbett is a humanist with the intermittent hobby of publicly debating local religious experts over the existence of God. The pro side points out that evolution—only a theory, they remind us—has not proved that men used to be monkeys. They declare that the existence of evil is proof of the Devil's existence, with the tacit assumption that only religion can induce moral behavior. The con side proclaims that modern biology proves that man is a product of natural selection and that altruism may be part of how our brains are wired to ensure species survival. This side also points out that the universe is about fourteen billion years old, the earth four billion, while humankind is maybe a million years old. Why the long wait to create us?

I was attracted for a time to Pascal's Wager (there is no harm in believing, even if you're wrong), but it seemed a disingenuous effort to fool an omniscient deity. So there I was, wandering toward my thirties, pondering how I could reconvert through a scientific understanding of God and everlasting life, and live in a way that would make me eligible to enter the Kingdom of Heaven without actually believing in Him.

It didn't seem evenhanded that I could live up to the standard that is promoted by every Christian, every other religion of Abraham, and probably most other religions in the world, yet not be bestowed that everlasting reward because I didn't have that final ticket—a belief that a God existed that had the desire and intent to condemn someone like me who was sincerely trying to do his best with this gift of life.

Buddhism and other exotic religions were attractive, but all suffered the same hard-to-believe conditions for final approval—you had to do silly things during your life to reach the ultimate goal. Chanting, for example. Chanting didn't seem to be the best use of my limited time on earth, or the most promising way to eternity. And what if you had to continue chanting all the time in order to stay up there? (Or maybe once through the Pearly Gates you can do anything you want?) No, thanks. There had to be something that made better sense and I had to find it. Maybe religion was a psychosocial need. So I took a psychosocial class, the Psychology of Religion. There were two major benefits from this experience: I became an agnostic for the next twenty years or so, and I learned about Viktor Frankl.

Viktor Frankl was an Austrian psychiatrist purported to be the heir apparent to Freud, rival of Jung and the originator of the third school of Viennese psychiatry. His claim to fame was the book, *Man's Search for Meaning*, based on what he saw and endured as a prisoner in Nazi death camps. He was trucked with thousands of others to Auschwitz before being hauled to Kaufering and then to Türkheim. His wife was moved in a boxcar from Auschwitz to Bergen-Belsen where she died. Frankl's mother and brother died at Auschwitz. Keep in mind these were normal, everyday people who had done nothing wrong, but were uprooted from their homes, forced into these death camps and systematically killed through starvation and beatings, by being crowded into gas chambers and by having to line up above open

trenches and be ripped apart by machine gun bullets...
in addition, of course, to impromptu executions in the
streets.

Doctor Frankl was someone who experienced firsthand
more death, more subjugation and more cruelty than
most modern humans, yet was able to find meaning in
those horrific circumstances. Unlike me, tormented
beyond reason after viewing a generic documentary
movie in a high school class, Frankl's entire world was
hopelessness. His life was controlled by forces that hated
his existence and that created daily tortures specifically
designed to break the spirit of the prisoners and hasten
illness and death. Each morning more bodies were found
among the sleeping, further eroding any sense of dignity
or personal control.

What did Doctor Frankl know that I didn't? He could
find meaning and recognize the soaring spirit of humankind even in a Nazi death camp. Me? I was having
trouble finding any kind of meaning in the good old U.S.
of A. Since I wasn't sure I had a God who afforded me
the luxury of a heaven in the sweet by-and-by, I had to
do the right thing in this lifetime and I had no clue what
that should be, and I worried that I might not be giving
God enough credit.

Nonbelievers isolate themselves. There is no club of
atheists who meet regularly to celebrate their nonbelief,
just as there is no group of lapsed Zeus or Thor wor-
shipers chatting about the old days. (Although some
atheists, to create a sense of community have begun

attending specially designed services sans the religious aspects.) Have you noticed how many religions seem to have faded away? Do religions die a natural death after a while? If the ancients had not worshiped gods, would we have one now? Of all the gods in history, did the best one win?

Nowadays, it doesn't seem like God has everyday management responsibilities like in olden times. He doesn't burn bushes or hand out tablets. Currently, He might have a laissez-faire approach. Maybe we should become godlike ourselves, defining our own morality. If enough of us believe that if we're nice to others, others will be nice to us, that might be enough to ensure a continuing world as good as the one we have now.

As I approached thirty, God was on the bench until I could trust that He was the only one who knew the rules of the game. I couldn't trust doctrine, didn't know what stories had what meanings, and had no compass to help guide me through all the available religious options. Can five billion believers be wrong? Absolutely, five billion believers can be wrong. Is life's meaning found only from a devout giving of one's self to an invisible Supreme Being through ritual, self-sacrifice, hymns and regular prayer? Put another way, does the God who created us, the one who can control all that we do, who can make anything happen, really have the need for us to worship Him? And also bribe us with favors and rewards to increase the probability of this worship?

What about prohibitions? No meat on Fridays? What was that about? No caffeine, beer, music or dancing? He seems needier and fussier than a God should be. Was this a celestial mystery or a manmade mélange of archaic ideas? To me it was a messy, jury-rigged, inconsistent, illogical, primitive, ever-changing, self-serving construction of His presence. Yet ultimate truth and meaning might be in there somewhere. But where?

~ Existence Precedes Essence ~

Frankl preached hope, but I figured that rebooting to the stance that life has no meaning seemed like a useful route to learn what I needed to know. At least it seemed better than deciphering fables and spending my allotted days chanting, singing, fasting and praying. My descent into life's meaninglessness began innocently enough.

I took French in school, from the seventh through the twelfth grade, with an average mark on my report card of C-, passing each semester only because the teachers recognized that I was trying my best. I took French because my sister took it and I hoped she would help me when needed, and because the nearest place where they spoke a foreign language was Quebec. Never did I imagine I would live for twenty years in Southern California where Spanish would have been handy, which I never learned either.

Graduating from college required two years of a language, achieved by passing a second year course. The professor was a passionate French existential philosophy fan and for me early in my search for the meaning of life, his timing and focus couldn't have been better.

First on the docket was Jean Paul Sartre and *No Exit* (in French, *Huis Clos*, which of course I read and didn't understand). The story is about three people stuck in a room with no exit. Near as I could figure, they're dead and in hell; the hell is that people are mere objects to one another. Each individual, a living, breathing *me* to themselves, is like furniture to the other two; that is, no connecting, no caring, no sense of belongingness, only emotional isolation for eternity.

We read a number of stories. (Are all routes to enlightenment and salvation through stories? Can't there be a scientific formula?) One short story affected me more than others but I have not been able to find it again. The story (as best I can recall) told of a man on a train, sitting comfortably in the lounge car, drinking sherry and reading a newspaper. The train is slowly ascending a long trestle. The man looks out the window, down to a stream far below and watches a boy playing near the water. Suddenly the boy slips on a rock and falls into the stream. He struggles to remain above water but soon loses the battle and drowns, all while the man watches from behind his newspaper and the comfort of his chair.

I devoured every assignment our professor gave us, attempting to glean as much knowledge from these stories as I did the Bible stories I learned as a child. I ended up learning a little French, a lot of existentialism and earned, by the professor's good graces, a gentleman's C. I could graduate.

Graduate school continued my good fortune. At this level, you needed two languages to earn a doctorate. One language, luckily, could be something like a computer language or statistics; this I could do. The second language, though, had to be a real language. There was no way I could succeed in a graduate level French class. The out was to pass a language competency test, in this instance translating an article from French to English, without the comfort of a dictionary, within a certain length of time; I think it was two hours. I signed up for the test; what did I have to lose?

If there was ever a sign from above, I was about to have that everlasting light shine on me. On the day of the exam, I sat down with a handful of other students in a windowless room, each of us at a desk with a typewriter. The professor walked to each desk and handed out the five-page article. Although I had not read this particular paper, I could tell it was on French existentialism. I couldn't decipher many of the words, but I was able to reconstruct what I guessed was the author's theme. I handed in my translation with not a small degree of optimism. Within a week I received a note that not only had I passed, but the examiner thought it was the best student translation he had ever seen. I had not simply restated the words in English; I had expressed the essence of the ideas. Hoo-ha!

Being exposed to existential philosophy in French class was a fortuitous accident and this new point of view contributed to my focus on philosophy as my initial search for a way to understand one man killing another. On my own I began reading the most famous philosopher I knew, Plato. I read his *Republic* and the allegory of the cave. I wasn't much interested in what beauty was or justice; I wanted to understand daily reality and what wisdom was, how to get it and how to use it. Plato's ideas were intriguing, but I drew more comfort from the fact that here was someone a couple thousand years before my time who was wrestling with similar issues.

I took a course in introductory philosophy that was also enlightening and comforting, but it wasn't until I discovered psychology that I realized there was actually a study of human behavior, not just the discussion of profound ideas. I needed both. It wasn't curiosity; I was floundering. And it seemed to me that the world was doing worse. The Vietnam War was displayed on the front page of the newspaper every day. The TV news reported body counts in the hundreds after every battle; usually the score was something like US dead: sixty-five; Viet Cong killed: seven hundred forty-four. I was 2-S with the draft board, meaning I was exempt from the draft as long as I was in school. But once graduated, I was certain to be drafted and most likely would be sent to the war. Some friends from high school were already in-country. I was lucky to attend college.

In psychology class I learned about Wilhelm Wundt and the first psychology lab in Leipzig in 1879. He was the first to define psychology as a separate field of scientific study. But that kind of information was not what I was looking for. Neither were James Watson and B. F. Skinner and their behaviorism. There was also Mesmer and animal magnetism in the eighteenth century, Freud and the unconscious, and then Jung with the collective unconscious. This was all intellectually interesting, but wasn't what I needed to know.

What I learned from my existential, semi-beatnik undergraduate studies was that I was responsible for figuring out the meaning of life. That wasn't much of a revelation; I had already started doing that. What helped was to find myself within a crowd of very smart people seeking the same thing, many of whom had found satisfactory answers.

My philosophical mentor is Michel de Montaigne, the sixteenth century French essayist. He was of a wealthy, well-established family, but was plagued by kidney stones and died young, at fifty-nine; not quite the ideal model of a life of meaning I was hoping for, but he taught me I didn't need a model. In his era he was a respected public official; to those of us who read his essays today, he provides critical insights into what it is to be human.

Simply put, Montaigne gave me permission to live my life as best as I could figure out. There were no experts on my life except me. He said, "The greatest thing in the world is to know how to belong to oneself." These thoughts are how I translated some of his ideas into my own life:

- There is no great truth to discover, we can know only of ourselves.
- Each of us has to find happiness in our own way.
- Pay attention and you will learn what you need to know.
- I will never learn enough to know enough, only to wonder.

As Montaigne and others influenced my thinking, I grew more confident that I would find what life is about and how to find the meaning I sought. No one person or creed or philosophy had all the answers and the more confident people and groups were about their particular way, the less likely it would be right for me.

Doctrine was the anti-answer. The more established and popular an approach to living was, the more I had to question it. Religion was becoming archaic, a primitive way of understanding nature—not the nature of man, nor my personal life and the meaning I needed to find. I was willing to accept the possibility that life didn't have meaning. Evolution strongly suggested that increasing the chances of survival of the species was the only life purpose for me and every other living thing.

Existence precedes essence; you have to exist before you can do something. The profound question is: do what? The existential position suited my scientific bent like a pet gold fish; too small and isolated to be an intimate companion, but interesting anyway. Maybe meaning is an illusion based on man creating a God powerful enough to demand it.

~ The Science of Human Behavior ~

I took my first psychology class in 1964 and have been studying this science ever since. Formally, I have a BA, MA and PhD, plus a year of predoctoral and another year of postdoctoral training. I've attended conferences, spoke at some, wrote a dissertation on psychotherapy, worked with hundreds of people, groups and businesses, and read countless journals. I know the field pretty well.

As an undergrad, I was most exposed to behavioral psychology. My primary interests at the time were neurophysiology and learning theory. Both areas were fascinating, but I couldn't work up enough interest to make either field a career.

Graduate school provided exactly what I was looking for. My first posting as a sailor was at the now defunct Miramar Naval Air Station maybe fifteen miles north of downtown San Diego. Despite being a highly trained uniformed protector of our freedoms, I was against war and expressed my feelings with a peace sticker on the front bumper of my car (who could be against peace?). I was stopped and hassled too many times at the front gate of the base so I moved the decal to the back bumper and was waved through every morning without further trouble.

Although I went home to civilian life every evening, my days as a military man were demoralizing. I had to salute officers, some of whom were as socially conscious as a Cape buffalo. I had to wear a hat if I went outdoors, which felt silly. And since I wore a work uniform on base that was not approved off base, I put civilian clothes over my uniform to drive on the base, then once I got to the squadron parking lot took them off while sitting in the car. Going through this process enabled me to avoid changing in the barracks, which gave me precious extra minutes of being a civilian. At my desk I had to answer the phone with a greeting that took about five seconds to say—something like, "Good morning, VF 435, operations department, Brown speaking, how may I help you, sir?" Most phones on base were answered with equally long greetings, but were said in two seconds and were unintelligible. I felt like an idiot taking the time to say mine so people could understand it. None of my military duties felt right. I was contributing to our country's napalm-fueled war machine, reluctantly and in a small way, but complicit nonetheless.

My war effort was to take IBM style cards (heavy paper about three-by-seven inches) speckled with squadron flight data like the amount of time the plane was flown, landing sites and fuel consumption, and transfer the number and letter codes to a large sheet of paper, one with rows of boxes that held the individual letters and numbers so they were easier for the data entry people to read. Basically, I defended our country by making it less likely for the input workers to make mistakes. That took two hours if I labored over each number and letter. Sometimes I alternated colors. For the rest of the day I had to look busy. One of my office coworkers was a verbal bully, mocking everyone he could, making snide comments and otherwise creating a workplace of open hostility; he also outranked me. The second was a bigot from South Carolina; he would tell stories of going nigger hunting from the bed of a pickup truck, swinging a long, heavy chain at any he saw. The office leadership, a navy chief, was primarily interested in chain-smoking cigarettes, sipping cold, black coffee and telling old navy stories. I was losing my mind.

I reported for duty in August; by September I was in desperate need of any kind of intellectual infusion and to do something, anything, I thought was productive. Being part of the Vietnam War was not why I got out of bed in the morning.

In perhaps the best bit of luck in my life, I read an article in the *San Diego Evening Tribune* announcing that no less than Viktor Frankl, MD, was going to be a visiting professor at a relatively new school, the United States International University (USIU), born out of California Western, a small but highly regarded private college. The concept was to create a truly international university with multiple campuses around the world. I believe there were five when I attended, including London, Nairobi and Mexico City. All I cared about was Professor Frankl.

I applied for the master's program in human behavior, was accepted and took a class with the esteemed professor. I wish I could say it revived my soul and fed my mind, but I don't remember. What I do recall of Dr. Frankl is his dignity and warm heartedness and that he called me by name when I raised my hand in class. Someone famous knew me! Most of the instructors seemed to be former chairs of psychology departments from around the country who'd retired to sunny Southern California and wanted to keep their hand in teaching, which meant the caliber of instruction was very high. In addition to Frankl, the school also brought in professors from other colleges, such as Herbert Blumer from Berkeley. They would fly in these part-time instructors to teach one three- or four-hour class a week. My boss, the story-telling chief encouraged me to attend school full-time and do my homework while on duty if I was able to look busy in the office; I couldn't read textbooks, but I could bang out papers on the typewriter. The navy paid for my master's degree, which I found ironic, but it was almost sadistic compensation juxtaposed with what the military was doing to me the rest of the time.

Typical of the dismissive attitude was what happened at a retirement ceremony for one of our squadron leaders. It was being held on a hot summer day. That morning I suggested to the commanding officer that I might disrupt the proceedings due to having orthostatic hypotension; I was one of those people who faint if they stand up too long, especially in hot conditions. He said, "Let's just see what happens." In the ranks of white uniformed sailors, in the middle of the ceremony, I fell forward onto my face. Blood was everywhere. People gathered around. The ambulance pulled up. After some delay I was carted off and the proceedings resumed. The next morning the commanding officer strode into my office, glared at me, but said nothing. I looked at him with as much innocence as I could muster, plus what I hoped was a look of expectation, maybe of an apology. Didn't get one, of course. He was a commander while I was a sailor—a puke, as we called ourselves. In combat, my rank and his attitude would have made me cannon fodder.

The emphasis at USIU was humanistic psychology, the third force; the first force is analytic (Freud and Jung) and the second, behavioral (Pavlov and Skinner). The analytic approach is based on drives, the effects of our basic biology, such as the pleasure principle and, of course, the famous conflicts between the id and the superego. Behavioral psychology is focused on how reward and punishment determine what we do. Humanistic psychology (led by such luminaries as Carl Rogers, Abraham Maslow and of course, Viktor Frankl, among others), has a different orientation:

- Humans are greater than the sum of their parts; people cannot be reduced to components.
- There is something we understand as the uniquely human context.
- Human consciousness is self-awareness and the awareness of others.

- Humans have choice, and thus responsibility.
- Humans are intentional, seeking value, meaning and creativity.

Talk about fulfillment; for eight to twelve class hours a week I explored what it was to be human, studied hard to understand human potential and shared ideas with equally motivated students and the absolutely best minds in the field.

One professor who had a strong impact was George Vlahos who later headed up the San Diego Institute for Logotherapy. Logotherapy was created by Dr. Frankl to help people find meaning in their lives. Dr. Vlahos created the four-question Logotherapy Test. I took the test in a class and sadly lost my original responses long ago, but immediately below are the questions and further below are my current answers.

> Who are you?
> Who are others?
> Why are you?
> Why are others?

Here are my current thoughts.

> Who are you?

>> I'm enjoying my days as an aging seeker of the meaning of life and I am a dedicated husband, father, grandfather, friend and

colleague. My primary job is being a good husband and the kind of Grampy my grandchildren desire and need. Selfishly, I'm taking a lot of time away from home chores to read and study as much as I can. And I am hoping I can live the best life for me and others.

Who are others?

Others are a curious mystery to me. All my life I have been fascinated by the many differences of others—their thoughts, art, music, feelings, cultural norms, religion, everything. I love the differences and learn so much by listening. By connecting with others, I make my life worth living. Others don't exist for me; I exist for them.

Why are you?

There is no why for me as an individual. I am a product of nature, the same as a stalk of corn, a blue whale or a cockroach. There is no why unless I create it. That's the meaning of it all.

Why are others?

My life could not have value without the existence of others. Others are my teachers and my companions on the walk through life. They are the history from which I grow and the future to which I want to contribute. In the present, others have wishes and needs I can meet, and they can say I love you when I feel alone and say thank you when I've contributed. Others are the reason to get out of bed in the morning.

Another lesson of perspective I learned during graduate school I read in the *Los Angeles Times*. The article was about a revered sports columnist who was about to retire. The interviewer mentioned the man's son was also a reporter, but he reported on important events, like politics. The sports columnist replied that sports were important on their own, but what his son reported on was significant. I've always tried to keep that concept in mind: minimize spending time on the unimportant, do what is important, but focus on what is significant. Significance is where true value lies.

Unimportant activities for me consist of watching TV, sitting in traffic, arguing to make a point, bad habits, worrying, shopping for clothes, playing video games and watering the lawn. You may disagree, of course.

Important activities include reading books, earning a living, giving to charity, being respectful to one another, being aware of and caring about your impact on the world, voting, helping children grow, doing chores, and parking within the lines. Feel free to disagree with these too.

Significant activities are righting wrongs, speaking up, making a contribution, understanding the big picture without losing the individual perspective, helping others succeed, taking chances to be yourself and leaving the world a better place. You may see this differently too.

The idea is to make decisions based on your values, not what seems useful at the time. You might value naps in a hammock over washing the car; that's fine. Watching TV because you can't think of doing anything better is a mistake. At least, I think it's a mistake. You have a limited amount of time and energy and you have no idea what tomorrow will bring. An old cliché we apply at our house is, "Make hay while the sun shines." Often that entails attending to less important outdoor work, like mowing the lawn before it rains again at our home near Seattle, Washington. Do the important, focus on the significant.

Sometimes what is significant isn't even important. What we're having for dinner is not important to me, but it is to my wife; that makes it significant. Same with tea parties; I can take them or leave them, but when my now six-year-old granddaughter wants to have a tea party, count me in.

Another experience of graduate school was to compose our own epitaph or what we'd like written on our tombstones. Along the same lines, we were asked to come up with our last words. All of it was the same for me; I wanted to connect with others, to touch and be touched. What is touch and be touched? It is people and what we mean to each other and how we fit in the world. Looking into a baby's eyes. Telling a difficult truth to a friend. Listening to my wife describe her day. The sound of a lonely clarinet, the imagery of a good poem and the eye contact when saying "thank you." It's trying to understand the cosmos. Sticking a hand into a cold mountain stream. Planting a bit of heather in the back yard. It's paying attention to the moment and giving a damn about being alive.

And I wanted my life to have some kind of purpose, in a sense making up for the lost life I observed five or six years earlier. It wasn't as if I had to live my life for the man who wasn't allowed to live his. My quest was to ensure I didn't waste the opportunity given to me. Learning psychology gave me a more scientific understanding of what it means to be human. Humanistic psychology, Viktor Frankl (among others) and the concepts of existentialism provided a context for me to understand *why* I must get out of bed in the morning.

It was up to me to figure out exactly what to do once my feet hit the floor, and now I had some solid ideas. Sort of.

~ Love, Family and Friends ~

Based on how well I turned out, my parents must have been wonderful at raising children. Other than occasional whippings with a leather belt, being slapped across the face by my grandmother and the time when my father deliberately dumped cold, wet, black gunk from our roof gutters onto my face because I wasn't moving fast enough with the trashcan, I was treated well.

According to family lore, my father quit school at fourteen and began work at the Glasgow shipyards on the river Clyde. Also according to family lore, this same Andrew Brown left Scotland at seventeen and arrived in New York City in 1930 with seventeen cents and two pencils in his pocket. A few years later he wrote to his girlfriend asking her to join him and start what became my family.

From the outset, Dad was desperate to overcome his Scottish upbringing and become an American. This quest eventually led him to lose a large chunk of his upper left arm in France during World War II. Like many vets of the era, he didn't talk much about his time in the war. Dad was usually cheerful, and able to do pretty much everything that needed to be done, from installing a bathroom in our basement to repacking the grease in the wheel bearings of our family car. His pleasures included golf and bowling, poker with the boys, bridge with other couples, reading, and watching the news and *Wide World of Sports* on television.

Mom was a bit sterner than my father but no less kind. Jeanne Redpath Barkley Kinloch Brown prepared grand holiday feasts for the family, made my lunches for school, rearranged our living room furniture seemingly every other week, was the primary helper with my homework (I can still hear her voice accenting some of the letters to help me spell a-r-t-i-f-i-c-i-a-l at the kitchen table), and took me and my brother to Hudson's department store in downtown Detroit for our new school-year clothes. This trip always included a cherished half-ounce bag of hot roasted cashews. Other shopping trips often ended with a hot fudge sundae at Sanders' lunch counter. With the sundae we would be served water in a paper cone tucked into a steel cone-shaped cup, the height of elegance to two elementary schoolboys.

I was lucky to have a sister almost three years older. Barb got into enough trouble, mostly with her choice of boyfriends, to keep what little heat I created from causing me any major problems. I was generally a good kid and didn't do much to worry my parents.

My poor brother Bill, almost five years younger, grew up with what I think were tired parents who gave him less support than he should have had and more criticism than he deserved, at least for his first dozen years.

Barb, being older and a girl, exposed me to a teenage culture that was a bit advanced for me, but naturally didn't include me in much of what she did. I wouldn't say we were close growing up, but she did create a little ceremony for when I decided to give my soul to Jesus. And although my brother and I shared a bedroom until my sister left when I was sixteen, Bill and I didn't get close either.

I had a few girlfriends beginning in junior high and continued through college with dates here and there, especially during summers when I worked as a lifeguard. For the most part, however, after being smitten in high school, I dated just one wonderful young woman. We married after college, but it wasn't a forever marriage as I thought it would be.

I've been married three times. This might make me a two-time loser but I now consider them practice marriages for the one that would finally stick. Besides my wives, there were a few other women who I also loved. One, maybe two of them, would have made me a happy husband.

As I mentioned, my first high-school sweetheart wife left me because she needed to find herself. The marriage was good, she said, and she loved me. She broke my heart and it was more than five years in the mending. If I had done something wrong I would have had a better chance of accepting this loss. Instead, what was most important to me walked away and there was nothing I could do to fix it—no thatched roof cottage, no white picket fence, no golden retriever lying at my feet.

Her need to redefine her life began when we backpacked in the Sierra Mountains. She tested herself in the wilderness, overcame challenges and liked what she was becoming. She sold our old sedan and bought a black Porsche 914, which she drove everywhere until it could go no more. After she left she sent postcards of her journey on the Silk Road in Asia and eventually moved to Katmandu. I think she found herself by exploring the world.

My second wife and I worked in the same office for a while. We dated and I slowly fell for her. I probably loved her family as much as I did her. She had two beautiful sisters, two handsome brothers, a society mother and a John Wayne dad. Her parents lived in a ten-thousand-foot multimillion dollar home in Rancho Santa Fe, which contained two golden retrievers each able to carry five tennis balls in its mouth. I loved going over there for cocktail hour, which seemed to be whenever I arrived. My second wife left me after seventeen months, realizing before I did that we were not well suited for the long run. She was right, but I was heartbroken to lose a little boy who had just started calling me "Dad." She did well after me too, marrying a chiropractor and graduating from law school.

My third and current wife of twenty-five years performs a daily miracle. Hubris or not, I didn't think anyone could be interesting to me after years of daily contact.

She is and I think she will continue to be immensely interesting and only becomes more so as I get to know her better. Searching for the meaning of life notwithstanding, my most contented moments are when I'm in the living room with a Scotch and a book and she is in the kitchen making something spectacular for us to eat.

In my fifteen years or so of single life between ages eighteen and forty-four, I probably went out with a hundred women. I disliked maybe two and I say two because I can remember only one I didn't like, but there must have been more than just the one. The majority I saw only once or twice, neither party sensing a true connection. The longer relationships I usually ended and did so poorly. I never knew how to avoid hurting someone, so I did what I could to explain that it wasn't her and it wasn't me, it was simply a matter of fit. It hurt anyway. I wish I could apologize for all the frustration, irritation or damaged feelings this probably caused.

One of my fondest memories as a single guy is the image of a golden-haired Southern California girl on a treeless mountain road in remote Peru, leaning over to talk in Spanish to a wide-eyed peasant boy of about six or seven. He may never have seen a blonde-haired person before and now one was talking to him in his own language, her hair blowing in the wind as she brushed it off her face in that way women do. They talked for five minutes or so and he stood watching our car until we drove over a rise and out of sight.

Laura was a special friend; we were a couple for a few years and traveled and spent a lot of home time together. I remember her making toast late one morning, which she served on her best china. I remarked that simple toast didn't warrant such fine treatment and she replied, "Things you use every day should be beautiful."

Unfortunately, Laura was also symbolic of the damage caused by my other quest, that of true love. She would have made a wonderful wife, but I didn't feel what I thought was absolutely necessary: the spark. One woman I dated, who once told me she wanted to have my children (which I took to mean she wanted to marry me), ridiculed my need for that spark, telling me I was being childish. When I tried breaking up with this woman, she would never accept what I was saying. I was stalked, smothered and manipulated. Usually it's men doing that to women. Athletes say they learn more from losing than winning. True, I must have learned four hundred and seventy-five lessons about men and women in that relationship. Lesson one was that an angelic face does not an angel make.

Laura, on the other hand, was everything any man could want. Even though I loved her and loved her son, I decided to end the relationship. It was too one-sided. I had an enjoyable companion while she banked her feelings hoping I would finally see the reality that she was the one. I knew I wouldn't ask her to marry me (although it was sorely tempting). I ended it badly, of course, but ending it was the right thing to do.

Looking back, I'm amazed women enjoyed spending time with me, especially romantically. Being only slightly above average certainly applied to my attractiveness to women. I was not great looking, not wealthy, not powerful, certainly not well dressed. I was not what most people would call a great catch. But I did have presence. I was there, listening, and was fascinated by their femaleness. Maybe that provided a good start.

I remember the initial kiss with a woman after my first wife left. She was a Jaclyn Smith lookalike, with the same flowing raven hair and a figure that was all woman. The kiss was enveloping; she gently sucked when she kissed, and after seven years of kissing the same woman, I was mesmerized by this exciting new, fully grown-up experience. That feeling continued with each woman I dated. I was surprised and flattered that they would give me so much of themselves.

My biggest mistake with women, as far as I can figure out, was not appreciating what it meant for them to give. I thought every relationship was fifty-fifty. That was my intent anyway. However, the reality was that I was being given more than I realized and was not giving back in proportion. Like so many men before me, I was simply enjoying myself while they were attempting to create a relationship.

For many of my single years I didn't want to be alone, but I didn't focus on finding another wife either. I was happy dating a lot of different women and enjoying many different experiences. At the time, I had no idea I was also being such a lousy son.

After graduating from high school I couldn't get out of the family home soon enough, but it took me two years of college before I finally left my childhood bedroom. Then, after college, when I was invited to join the armed services, my parents gave me and my bride the car we used to finally drive out of Dodge. We were off on the adventure of moving from rusting Detroit to suntanned San Diego half a continent away, maybe forever, while our respective parents, waving good-bye, were having their hearts twisted and wrenched as we drove out of their lives. I had no clue.

Later, as a single man, I introduced my parents to a number of women, some with wonderful kids who would make perfect grandchildren, who I whisked out of the picture with nary a thought. When I lived with my parents for a short time, I could be gone for a day, sometimes two, without a word. When I lived nearby I would visit sometimes, long enough for a sandwich, but no longer than it took to eat it and finish a drink. I wouldn't share much about my personal life, which was probably something they'd have loved to know about. When I housesat for them once and the house was burglarized I finally realized how vulnerable they had become and suggested we combine resources and buy a big house together.

My parents and I bought a house on top of a hill in La Costa. It was almost overwhelming luxury, especially for my dad who always tried to make do with the cheapest of alternatives. My mother adjusted well, enjoying decorating large sunlit rooms and cooking in a kitchen three times the size she was used to. After my father died, I made one of the worst decisions of my life, having my soon-to-be third wife move in with my mother and me. Absolutely everyone told me it would be a mistake. I thought otherwise—both women loved me, I loved both women, so what if they would have to share me, the kitchen, the living room, decorating schemes and quiet Sunday mornings? It didn't work, of course. My girl and I moved out, found a new place for my mother, sold the house, my mother moved to Georgia to be near my sister, and my new wife and I moved to Scotland—all pretty much because I tried to fit too much into the dream home.

I told my parents often that I loved them. Ignorantly, I didn't act that way at times, but I take a lot of comfort knowing that I expressed my love and appreciation every way I could and am sure they felt it.

Currently I connect with my sibs maybe once or twice a year, if that, and mostly by email. My sister had envisioned me as a close brother and a warm, caring uncle to her three daughters. It didn't happen. Same with my brother; we'd shared a room growing up, but were never close and still don't connect as well as would be nice.

I love them in my brotherly way; they are family and I know them well, but I don't feel a strong affiliation. I don't feel obligated to family. I don't feel much obligation to friends, either. I'm fair, I contribute, I easily go out of my way when asked and don't need others to reciprocate. I certainly don't reach out, make a call or send an email.

Jim, the fellow who dated my estranged wife and who I later joined in a medical practice, is in a different category. I have become part of his and his wife Tricia's family. This is a typical story about my good friend. In the late 1990s, my wife and I were living on Lone Lake, a near-circular lake about half a mile in diameter on Whidbey Island, Washington. Our house was a cabin with a huge back deck overlooking our yard, which sloped to the shore maybe a hundred yards away. We had a dock and a rowboat. That spring, two proud Canada geese parents showed off their eleven chicks by strutting around our yard before taking to the water. Each day we anxiously counted the chicks and each day there were eleven. One day, weeks after they first arrived, we counted eleven now almost full-grown grown offspring and never saw the family again. We were, however, visited by eleven mature birds a few weeks later and after that, thirteen sometimes arrived, sometimes more.

During our geese-counting time, I was laid off due to budget cuts and we were hurting. The phone rang almost every evening with someone demanding a payment. On the ferry coming back from the unemployment office, I stood by the rail watching the water. I thought about George Bailey, the main character in *It's a Wonderful Life*. His financial troubles took him to the rail of a bridge where he watched the water and thought about jumping in, his life insurance making him better off dead than alive. I didn't think about jumping in, I was just thinking about George Bailey jumping in. I didn't have life insurance.

When I arrived home, there was a letter from Jim. I opened the envelope and read his note: I could take what he sent as a gift or a loan or however I chose. Inside was a check for a thousand dollars. I don't know how he knew of our pressures, but the money paid our rent, got us current on bills, and provided relief and hope. I accepted the money as a gift, one that I would reciprocate someday.

A few years later, the advance for one of my books gave me enough to return that thousand dollars to him.

Not reaching out might be why I currently have few close friends. I've had many golfing buddies over the years, but there were few occasions where we would do anything other than play golf together. Only two or three guys might come over in a household emergency. This feels okay to me. I love spending all the time I have with my wife.

I'm not much of a father figure. My two almost middle-aged stepchildren clearly see me as a nice stepfather, but they already have a serviceable father and I'm mostly an appendage attached to their mother. But, grandfather? That's where I can shine. I'm the one grandfather out of three who lives near enough to have a good connection with the young ones. Nothing is better than kneeling down as they dash toward me and feeling their skinny arms wrapping around my neck. My job, as I see it, is to spoil them rotten while teaching them the rules of life. I can spoil them too much, but I will never be able to listen enough. I want to join them in their world and give them peeks at mine.

However, overall I'm an isolated guy, somewhat by design. I don't need anyone. I want my wife, but don't need her. I want my children and I want my grandchildren. My guess is that if my wife dies and I'm still around, I won't last long. Maybe that's a need, but I don't see it that way. Life is a choice; it's not a *have to*. I choose to live because I like my life and I like my wife and family, and because what I do adds meaning to my getting out of bed in the morning. Family and friends are important, but not necessarily significant. But love, the way I have been lucky enough to experience it, that's really something.

Just as I had no idea how totally enrapturing grandchildren would be, I truly didn't learn about love until maybe fifteen years into my current marriage. Like most people, I thought I knew what love was; I felt it, acted on it, enjoyed it.

I was walloped over the head on the first date with my wife, as if Cupid had a rubber mallet in addition to his arrows, just for such existential moments. I asked her about marriage ninety minutes into our date. I didn't call her after our first dinner for a week. I was overwhelmed and basically couldn't think. I needed a week to come to grips with the fact that this woman was different and exactly what I wanted. However, that immediate infatuation grew into a love of a different kind.

At times during our first fifteen years, I entertained the idea of life without my wife. We had our squabbles and outside stresses that made the single life look easy and attractive, at least in concept. I don't think I would ever have actually moved out and didn't come close to doing that. In the last decade or so, a deeper love emerged. Doing things my way became less important. Listening—always one of my strengths—became more acute. I tried harder to listen and heard more—the depths of her opinions for one and the meaningful details of her day for another—and fell in love in a more substantial way, different from any feeling I've experienced before.

The feeling began from our living together, relating and simply being adjacent to one another. There was watching her in action, interacting with our family, friends and even strangers in the grocery store. She would see someone in the parking lot struggling to put bags in the car and help out, and then return their grocery cart to the store for them. Respect must be a large chunk of love.

After fifteen years I understood what the word "us" could mean.

Answering the proverbial question of how much do you love me, giving up my life to save hers is nothing. What is profound is not *giving up* my life, but *giving* my life to her, a more difficult and more telling effort. The difficulty comes from being true to myself and to her, with being true to her the more complicated consideration. If I simply said, "Yes, dear," at every opportunity, that wouldn't do. That would disrespect both of us. When she wanted my opinion, I had to be honest with her. She, after all, married me for a reason. I had to make sure to continue being a good reason to stay married, and as she continues to improve as my wife I want to continue to improve as her husband.

Guessing how to be a good husband is a mistake many husbands make. None of us can guess that well. When I practiced marriage counseling estranged husbands would ask me what they could do to win back their dissatisfied wives. I suggested they ask their wives and do what the wives wanted them to do. Most husbands complained that the wives wanted less pressure to get back together and more time to sort out their feelings. The men didn't want to do that and were soon pressuring their wives to come home, and these men almost always lost out.

This deep love that I have learned must come after a long period of sharing. I don't think it's complex or mysterious. Most older couples probably enjoy the feeling. Like wisdom and a smooth Scotch, it's yet another of the gifts of time.

Romantic love, according to some, is made up of passion, commitment and intimacy. For me, it began with passion, which remains a driving force. I couldn't keep my eyes off her and couldn't stop thinking about her or leave her alone. Commitment, fragile at times, has become as hard and stable as granite. It would take circumstances I couldn't imagine for me to leave. The best part of love for me is the intimacy. I think of it as she being my other half, trite as that may sound. She means more to me than me. Together we are more than the sum of our parts. She lights my fire, lights my way and lights the darkness that sometimes comes over me. I like listening to her and I like the questions she asks me. The only thing better in my life than just sitting next to my wife is holding her hand.

I was at a party a few years ago, and, as is usual for me at a social function, asked the woman I had just met what she thought the meaning of life was. Without hesitating she said, "Love." I think that is a superb one-word answer; maybe it's even *the* answer. It certainly makes life worth living. Love. What can be more important than love?

~ Dreams ~

To sleep, "perchance to dream. Aye, there's the rub..." Dogs chase squirrels in their sleep. I imagine cats dream about napping. Freud thought dreams were the royal road to understanding the unconscious mind. But for the most part, sleeping dreams are simply the brain entertaining itself with little or no psychological secrets being expressed or explored. All the real action is in daytime dreaming.

Dreams we create when awake take us to the land of possibilities, no matter how remote. All of us have dreams, only a few pursue them, and fewer yet come close to living them. It all depends.

My brother is a dreamer. Like most, he has not come close to realizing the big ones. Also like most people, he never went beyond the dream stage and probably never believed he would. Some dreamers know only how to dream. Living the dream is impossible for them; they are not up to the task, they have limited opportunities, they have bad luck, they make bad choices. Life is but a dream. The rest of us have to figure out how to give dreams a decent chance at life.

My sister is a dreamer and is close to living her dream. She has been married to the man she loves for fifty years. She had a dream job as a teacher and won the state teacher of the year award. She has three delightful daughters who have provided her with a handful of equally delightful grandchildren.

My parents were dreamers, leaving Scotland to chase the American dream, and I believe they thought they were successful. In Scotland it would have been tenement housing, my mother would have been a homemaker and my dad some kind of laborer. Instead they owned a three-bedroom brick home, drove a four-door American sedan, went on annual vacations and retired to California before my dad turned sixty-five.

I'm a dreamer too, but maybe different from those in my family and others I know. Some of my dreams are odd. Psychology has a clever concept that we contain three selves: our real self, our social self and our ideal self. My principal dream had to do with my ideal self becoming my real self, which also would be my social self. At first this particular dream was impossible to reach. My social self was primarily shy and insecure, which often was expressed by what looked like aloofness. My real self you already know—pretty nice, above average, nothing special. My ideal self early on was the English gentleman, a combination of Richard Burton, James Bond, Jeeves the butler, David Niven and Cary Grant. I would have been soooo cool. My current dream for my three selves is to be gracious in all circumstances.

Melding my three selves would enable me to create a true intimacy with others, to touch and be touched in the most meaningful ways. I feel this possibility when I say good-bye after a visit from my three-year-old grandson. He will be sitting in his car seat, a closed window between us. One of us will touch the window with an index finger and the other will do the same so the tips are only a glass width away from each other. I have no idea what he is thinking. My dream is that I will connect with those I like and love in a way that may be impossible to measure, but that is truly human.

More common dreams were to have a doctorate and a judo black belt by the time I was thirty; I got the doctorate, and was just about awarded a brown belt when I stopped doing judo. Travel dreams included sticking my hand in the Amazon River, walking on a glacier, trekking up to the base camp on Mount Everest, snorkeling around the Great Barrier Reef, visiting a Japanese temple, playing golf on the Old Course at St. Andrews, Scotland, exploring Machu Picchu and trudging on the snow in Antarctica, among another dozen or so. I haven't made it to Antarctica yet, and I think I've erased Everest from my list. I'm close to taking a cruise through the inside passage to Alaska which has been on my dream list for a long time.

My life hasn't included more expansive dreams, like becoming a millionaire, but I hoped to create something that would enable people to live better lives. I did that for individuals and families as a clinical psychologist and for businesses as a consultant. My major, although little known, contribution to humankind is a five-step process (Harnessing the Speed of Thought®) which enables people to solve problems with their collective brainpower rather than debating which approach is best. My way enables groups to assemble solutions. (If you want to learn how this works, it's explained in *Transparent Management*.)

For me, dreams have been like salt and pepper, spicing my life with what made getting out of bed more interesting than it otherwise would have been. Work, of course, was rewarding, but dreams meant that tomorrow held a promise I could pursue.

Paul Plsek is an expert on business innovation who advocates three steps to finding better ways of doing things: attention (fully understand what you want to improve), escape (find new ways) and movement (go beyond the bounds of normal thinking). When I teach this concept, I ask people to look at a common red brick and understand how it is used in construction. This is the attention step. Then I ask them to think of five non-construction uses of bricks. Usually people think of using them to line flowerbeds or maybe plopped into a toilet water tank to reduce water use. However, this step still uses a brick as a three-dimensional object. Movement means to go beyond normal usage, like chipping the brick into pieces that could be used as coins or using brick dust to make paint. Dreams can be conceptualized the same way. Understand what you want, create ways of reaching for it and continue to find newer and better ways of achieving it.

If you truly understand yourself, pipe dreams are of no interest. Dreams of vast riches, becoming a movie star or winning the Indy 500 are of little use because they have no relevance. Grandiose dreams are really just fantasy. The real action is dreaming about a Duke Snider baseball mitt at age ten and saving up allowance and birthday money to finally stride into the sports department at Montgomery Ward, lift the mitt out of a basket of dozens of others and smelling the leather and sticking your hand into it every step of the way home.

At twenty-five it was dreaming about earning a PhD and opening up a psychology practice. In my mid-forties it was making a major contribution to improve how people solve problems together. Now my dream is to write twenty books, maybe have one of my movie scripts filmed or the play performed, to visit the Grand Canyon with my wife, to have a positive impact on my grandchildren and to die well.

Dreams are directions rather than outcomes. I may not publish more books, but I intend to write them. My wife and I may not make it to the Grand Canyon, but maybe we'll take a few extra trips to Cannon Beach, Oregon. We won't be able to do all we dream about; a rail trip across Canada to the Canadian Maritimes probably won't happen. How much does achieving a dream mean? Not much.

Dreams are different from goals. Dreams include an element of chance and a touch of wonderment, whereas goals, properly set goals, can be achieved with the right decisions and the necessary work. We don't have much control over reaching our dreams. Achieving a dream can be considered a gift. One of my dreams is to live in an elegant house with a view over Puget Sound shipping lanes and the Olympic Mountains. I'm doing nothing to achieve this dream except buy an occasional Mega Millions lottery ticket.

A mentor of mine once described me to a mutual friend as an idealist. This mentor is a hard-nosed executive and occasional high-ranking member of the federal government. The description wasn't a compliment, but I took it as one. An idealist is a kind of dreamer. Goal setters may get more done, but idealists, dreamers, they make the great leaps.

Thomas Edison was a success-driven goal setter who transformed the world. I think Nelson Mandela was a dreamer, someone with a vision, who had a strategy, but the quest was a never-ending process of stretching toward what is right. I like to think dreamers have the good of mankind in their hearts.

We humans have been blessed with an imagination, the ability to travel throughout the universe and backward and forward in time. It is a great gift. We can visualize becoming anything we want. I believe that self-awareness is the best way to define the boundaries of our lives. And I believe that dreams enable us to continually push past those boundaries.

It should go without saying, but I'll say it anyway: without dreams all we would be doing is responding to changes in our environment, as those behaviorists say we do. But we know that people can create the future. The current expression, "It is what it is," accepts reality, which is good. But what about saying, "It isn't what it could be?" This is about attitude. Dreams are the stepping-stones to the best we can be; as individuals and as societies. "Life can be a dream," and a dream can become a life.

~ Life ~

L ife is how we invest our available time. What happens during this time constitutes living. Many people have had thoughts about it: "Life, what a concept!" (George Carlin originally said, "Reality, what a concept.") "As good an idea as any." "What to do until you can think of something better." "Life is what happens while you're busy making other plans." And (a bit of a negative point of view), "...it's ending moment by moment." And another favorite, "It's what happens between innings."

Unfortunately, or perhaps fortunately, we must earn our way through life. Once we leave the subsidy of our parents, we have to sustain home and hearth. How we choose to earn a living, how we respond to the day-to-day circumstances we encounter, whom we share life with and how well we manage our free time are the fundamental issues.

I've had tedious jobs: spot welder on an assembly line, manager at a drug abuse clinic and consultant to control-freak managers. I've had profoundly rewarding jobs: clinical psychologist, consultant to public service agencies, writer and teacher. My life plan has been to avoid a common forty-hour workweek as a cog in the wheel of a soulless organization, to avoid bosses who are dumber than I am and to always earn my living doing something I loved while leaving time to explore the world. That hasn't always been possible, but I've managed to do it enough that I'm still able to live my desired work-and-explore-the-world life, earning a bit of money and doing what I believe is worthwhile.

Certainly I am privileged to love what I do and be able to pay the bills. Most people could do the same, but get distracted by other values, like making lots of money, maximizing security, enjoying nice vacations and driving a car with a working air conditioner. My wife and I live in a modest house, make about the average household income, and haven't had a vacation longer than three days in twenty years. Yet she is working in her almost dream job and I am working in my dream job and we couldn't be happier.

Twenty years ago, we quit our jobs, and sold our house, furniture and cars to move to Scotland. We sold our house in a down market, had no jobs when we returned, lost more than a hundred thousand dollars with the move away and back, and we'd do it again in a heartbeat. People ask how we had the courage to take such a chance. It isn't a matter of courage, but of perspective. As an answer to their question, all we can do is shrug our shoulders and say, "That's what life is for." I think we have our priorities right.

As a consultant to businesses, I often ask management if they know the individual mission statements of their employees. Usually I need to explain the idea that people come to work with a conscious or unconscious definition of how to achieve personal fulfillment from their work. This outcome can range from doing as little as possible and still receive a paycheck to trying hard, learning important skills and moving up the organizational ladder. I ask managers to learn the missions of their employees so they can help employees fulfill them, which in turn can help the company fulfill its own mission.

My work mission is short-term. I hope to end each day with my client saying, "Thanks Bob, I can do my job so much better now." Part of this mission arose during graduate school when I learned the concept of worth and worthiness. The idea is that every living thing has worth; being alive makes it so (some say only humans have worth). A second concept, worthiness, is a feeling that can fluctuate depending on how we are treated. If people are supportive, we enjoy a strong sense of worthiness. When we fail or are treated poorly, our sense of worthiness falls. The worst case is when worthiness is so beaten down that our sense of worth begins to diminish too. My mission is to add to people's feelings of worthiness and to strengthen their sense of worth.

An additional concept that completes this idea is value. People may have worth, they may have a sense of worthiness, but do they have value?

Having value as a human is simply improving the life of other living things, even in a small way. I think most people have value, but they don't add as much value as they tend to take for themselves. Here's a common slice of how people often converse that makes the point:

She: Just got back from Hawaii and had the most wonderful time. We went wind surfing and hiking and had dinner just off the beach. We went snorkeling and...

He: Did you snorkel off Kauai? We did that in the morning and late that day played golf on the most wonderful course. You wouldn't believe...

She: We don't play golf but did spend some time at a club playing tennis. Golf takes too long and an hour of tennis left us enough time to watch the sunset while having drinks on our hotel veranda.

He: Tropical drinks. Aren't they wonderful? We...

Typical conversation, isn't it? Neither enhanced the other; neither asked expanding questions; neither made the effort to truly share the experience. Listening is done politely only until there's an opening to talk about you. The same perspective exists for every type of people interaction. *I am the center of the known universe* guides everything we do. If you think about it, though, this perspective is not selfish. It's understandable and absolutely true. What else could be the center of the universe except our individual point of view? The center of the universe is not our country, the earth, our sun, our galaxy, the most massive black hole known or any other physical entity. There is no actual physical center of the universe. Thus the only reasonable center of the universe is you—and me—and each of us all at the same time. We are all the center of our own universes. Each of us can, in a sense, create our own laws of time and space. Our personal universes are how we spend the time, the people we know, what we want, the rules we follow and our effect on others. You can decide if you want your universe to be positive, expanding for your benefit and the benefit of others. Or you can create a negative universe, one that consumes resources, sucking the energy and value from others. We have to be careful when our universe comes into contact with other universes. Given that we occupy the same space on occasion, we need to be kind to one another.

Being kind adds value; being angry, mean, critical, or selfish subtracts value.

The question for me and the question each of us should be asking is: what value am I adding? It doesn't take much to be a value contributor over the short run, but how much and what quality value are we adding throughout our lives and can we, should we, do more?

I add value in small doses. I'm nice to others as much as I can be. I listen when people talk to me and ask questions. I volunteer at a nonprofit and contribute to charities. I wish I could add more value, on a larger scale, like a surgeon who saves lives every day or a biochemist who invents a wonder drug. There are CEOs who create thousands of jobs and generals who win wars. I do what I can and am content with that. I figure that what I might lack in grandeur I can make up for in quality.

When I was a psychologist I wanted to never turn anyone away for an inability to pay. Yet I got busy, and one day a fellow who didn't have a job and didn't have insurance wanted an appointment. My front office suggested that he be referred to a nearby low-fee clinic and I agreed, and have regretted that decision ever since. My philosophy meant accepting patients who paid me in chocolate chip cookies or sometimes not at all. I might have been losing money, but I was adding important value, and that was what I wanted to do. In my universe, life is for adding value.

~ Death ~

Life is a butterfly fluttering high among light-dappled trees. Death is the cold miles deep in a blue-green ocean. Life is potential. Death is the end of possibilities. I used to think life and death were opposites. But I was wrong. Life and death are not opposites. They're not even related.

Death is the second half of nothingness. Meaningful human life begins at the instant of self-awareness and ends with the loss of self-awareness. Measures of life such as heartbeat and brain activity are relevant only for the biological human. Understanding human life and death must include what makes us an individual, not just an amalgam of cells with a first and last name.

After the shock of seeing the pilot executed in the film, my first direct contact with death was when my boyhood neighbor, Alan, was killed in an auto accident while serving in the navy. He was probably nineteen. I attended his funeral, for the first time standing next to and looking down at an actual dead body. His parents sat stone-faced off to the side of the casket, almost unresponsive to the people around them. The air was perfumed with sadness.

A few years earlier my mom's mother died and I was home with her when the telegram arrived. I did my best to console her as she sat on her bed trying not to cry. I offered to call the bowling alley where my dad was playing in his league. My mother said, "Don't, you'll put him off his game." My grandmother had lived with us when I was young, but I'd last seen her about seven or eight years earlier, so her dying didn't have much direct impact. Neither did Alan's death. I didn't like him and I hadn't seen him in a few years either. I felt bad for his parents. It seemed like he was all they had, and he hadn't done much for them to be proud of. He was a spoiled kid, so I suppose that made it worse for them; they couldn't prop him up anymore.

I obsessed about death throughout my young adulthood. Late at night I'd lie on my bed and wonder about dying. My heart would race. My breathing became quick and shallow, the room seemed to darken, even my skin tingled. The feeling of powerlessness was overwhelming. Death was evil, uncaring, relentless. I knew this specter was inexorably moving closer to me even in those moments. There was nothing I could do to stop my dying whenever death had the whim to walk up and tap me on the shoulder.

I wasn't afraid of dying. The possibility of being in pain wasn't pleasant. I didn't worry too much about not existing because I couldn't conceptualize such a state. What was horrible was the inevitability. I was going to die. I had to die. No choice, no chance. This night terror seized me every few weeks.

I first experienced total helplessness when my father died. He was dying in front of me and there was not a goddamned thing I could do to stop it. I loved my father. He was a good man. His first job after emigrating from Glasgow at seventeen was to work as a houseboy where his aunt Jean also worked—the home of Professor and Mrs. Trumbull on Washtenaw Avenue in Ann Arbor, Michigan. That was in 1931. Thirty-seven years later, I filled the same position in the same house for the same woman when I was a senior at the University of Michigan. I imagine I did the same kind of work for my room as he did—raking leaves, shoveling snow and running a sweeper over the ancient oriental rugs.

My dad had abilities beyond my ken. He could remember people's names years after he last saw them, play the piano and accordion by ear and compete in Master's bridge tournaments. I can do none of these things. After years of expressing himself with typical British reserve, he learned how to hug and to cry without shame. I may have enabled him to do some of that, of which I am very proud.

Instead of retiring to Florida like most Michiganders, my dad and mom moved to Del Mar, California, down the street from me, then to a new condominium in Cardiff-by-the-Sea. This was where they were living when their place was burglarized. I can still see my dad sitting in a lawn chair outside the La Costa house we bought together, sweeping the hose back and forth to water the plants in the front walkway. I was with him as he slowly succumbed to chronic lymphocytic leukemia, when he went by ambulance to the ER, and I was there when he came back from his last trip to Georgia to visit my sister. He hugged me and cried at the airport when he left and hugged me and cried when he returned.

My dad thought he would live to be eighty-one. He died at seventy-six. I was forty-three when he died, well into middle age and well into the life stage when I could expect to lose my parents as part of the natural course of things.

On a Friday, a home nurse took a sample of my father's blood and sent it to the lab. That Sunday night we had to call an ambulance, I think for the third time during the course of his disease. I followed the ambulance to the hospital where I was a consultant and thus had immediate access to the emergency room. Two attendants were lifting my dad from the gurney to a bed. He gestured for me to help them. I told him no, that they knew what they were doing and I would be in the way. That was the last time I could have helped my dad. I returned home and then to work while he was being shifted to the hospital that was covered by his health insurance. My mother monitored his arrival at the other hospital and when we would be able to see him.

Midmorning I received the message to call home immediately. My mother told me that the hospital said we should go there right away. We arrived to see my father in some distress, twisting about the bed as if he couldn't get comfortable. My mom and I sat at the end of his bed and watched as the staff cared for him. After fifteen minutes or so, a doctor motioned for us to follow him outside the room. We stood with him and he said, "I don't know if you realize this or not, but Mr. Brown is dying." We didn't realize it. How would we know that? We reentered the room and went back to sitting at the end of the bed, holding hands, again watching the staff take care of my dad. We didn't know what else to do. Within a few minutes, the doctor leaned over and placed his stethoscope on my dad's chest, stood up and said, "He's gone." My mother raced over to my dad's side, grabbed his arm and pleaded with him not to die. "Oh, Alec. Oh, Alec," she cried, until a nurse took her away from my dad to sit back in the chair next to me.

Later, while my mother sat alone in a little alcove, I signed the necessary paperwork, then we left my dad and went home. We drove along familiar roads, stopped at traffic lights and used the automatic garage door opener when we arrived at the house, as if this was just another day. We were numb. Nothing was real; nothing, absolutely nothing, mattered. Dad didn't come home with us as he always had before; he was never coming home. He was never coming home. One of my professors in graduate school told us he didn't understand the word never until his wife died. Never. Never. Never. Never. Never. Never. Never. I hadn't understood the word either.

Ten minutes before his death, my dad was talking to the medical staff while we looked on. He was a living person, although uncomfortable. Five minutes before he died, when he was dying, my dad was lying quietly. I assume his mind was on himself, focused on physical sensations. His eyes were closed and he wasn't paying any attention to us. Then he was dead, his body was still; my dad was gone.

After my mom recovered from trying to revive my dad, as she was being led to a quiet area, she turned and told me to get my dad's watch off his wrist. I'd never touched a dead body before. I looked at his hands. When I was young, his hands were strong, tanned, with dark hair on his fingers. I wondered then if my hands would eventually look like his. As he aged, his hands went from bronze to a pinkish blue with liver spots, as my hands are now. My dad's physical presence was important to me. He was disappointed to end up less than six feet tall; growing over six feet was something I was proud to achieve. His eyes were the clearest blue I can remember. I thought he was a handsome man, something I hoped to be. Now he was lifeless. I was alone in a room with my dead father and I was to touch his arm and take his watch.

My first impulse was to ignore my mom's request. Then I thought this was my dad, my mom wanted to keep his watch. How could I not touch him and get it for her? I touched his forearm, lifted it up and pulled off the watch. His skin was still warm, but it didn't feel like I was touching my dad's arm. There was no dad there; the arm was just an arm. I laid it down and put the watch in my pocket. My mom was waiting somewhere. Until her final hospitalization, she wore that watch every day.

Sometime that first afternoon, my friend Jim called and asked what he could do. I told him to call me every day. He did. The call lasted maybe five seconds. All I said was, "Hello." He said, "Hi Bob. I'm calling," and then I said, "Thank you," and hung up, but those calls told me that a world still existed somewhere.

Within weeks of my father's death, my mother and I decided to buy a new refrigerator and put in French doors to our back patio. Psychologists would call that "undoing," trying to make things feel okay again. I said to my mother one evening, "Well, you still have me." She tried to smile and with the saddest eyes I have ever seen, replied, "If I could choose..." A son sacrificed at the altar of more than fifty years of love. I wasn't offended and I truly believe she meant it.

My helplessness to save my father was offset a little by supporting my mother. I did my best to do for her while helping her do for herself. A typical learning event was filling her car with gas. She learned to do that and was quite pleased, against a backdrop of loneliness, hopelessness and an unrelenting sense of loss.

Within a year of losing my father, a long-term lady friend of mine ended her life. We were friends with benefits before the term was invented; I liked her a lot. She'd moved away a few years earlier to marry someone I didn't know but was back in town and had called me on a Monday to meet for lunch on Wednesday. My schedule was disrupted so I left a message on her answering machine telling her we needed to postpone.

The next day she ended her life. I couldn't get myself to attend her memorial service. Twenty-five years later I still wish she had waited until we could talk. I may have been able to save her. But maybe she didn't want me to. It doesn't matter. She's dead and isn't missing anything. But I miss her.

Fourteen years after my father died and across the country in a private room in a hospital in Dalton, Georgia, I held my mother's hand as she died. She was eighty-seven. She had been in and out of hospital for a few years. My sister, brother and I wondered about moving her from a two-bedroom apartment to a nursing home. We were all in town for her most recent hospitalization, not that we thought this one was any more serious than the others.

My brother had to attend a function out of town while my sister took care of family business. That left me with my mother for the morning. She was resting comfortably in her bed and we talked about the possibility of her being discharged the next day. Breakfast came but she only picked at it. I put earphones on her so she could listen to my iPod. After a minute she shook her head and I took it away. She didn't look good; her breathing was forced.

A nurse came in. My mother complained about her breathing and was given a pill. The nurse said it would take a few minutes to take effect. I sat on the window ledge looking down on her as we waited for her to feel better.

After a few more minutes she seemed to doze off. I went to her bedside and sat down. I held her hand and told her that she would soon feel better. Her breathing became more labored. She didn't open her eyes as I talked to her.

As my father weakened, the doctor had asked him if he wanted heroic efforts made to save him. Dad nodded toward us and said, "Let them decide." When the moment came and the doctor looked over, I shook my head, no.

Now I wondered if my mother was actually dying and what I should do. I could run for the nurse and maybe heroic efforts would be made. Or I could stay with her and hope for the best or watch her die if that was what was happening. I continued holding her hand and telling her that the medicine would soon be working. Without opening her eyes, she said, "I can't take this anymore." It wasn't a complaint as much as a statement of fact.

Her breathing continued to slow. I stopped talking and held her hand, thinking about her and thinking about my dad. Eventually her breaths were five or six seconds apart, slowed even more and then stopped. I held her hand for a while before moving back to the windowsill. Holding her dead hand reminded me of taking my father's watch. This time there was no discomfort. I sat there looking at her for ten minutes or so until a nurse came in, looked at my mother, looked at me, then wordlessly left.

A physician came in, examined my mother, looked at the clock, made a few notes and left (I can't recall if he said anything either). A couple of attendants soon arrived, straightened out the covers on the bed and basically laid my mother out for viewing, placing a rolled-up towel under her chin to keep her mouth closed. My sister and her husband came in and the rest of the day began.

For fifty years since that day when I was seventeen and saw the pilot fall, I've tried to understand life and death. I finally have. Unlike what I have always thought, life and death are not a continuum. Life and death are not opposites. They are like fish and chips—together, but with no connection with one another. It was religion that combined the two.

Religion is a prescientific attempt to understand the everyday world, first explained by attaching a god or spirit to events, natural flora and fauna, and the human condition. Thousands of years ago religion handled death by promoting an afterlife that seemed to make venerating one or more deities worth the effort. Reliance on the supernatural and a life after death created language that obscures what being dead actually is.

There is life and there is death, the assumed continuum being that one is born, lives, dies and becomes dead. In reality, before birth and after dying, there is nothing. Joe can die, but Joe cannot be dead. There is no Joe to be dead any more than there is a Joe before Joe is conceived. Our language leads us to believe that Joe can be in a state called dead which makes being dead unpleasant. We don't want to be in the state of dead; that doesn't sound nice at all. But there isn't a problem. The only state Joe can be in is alive. He cannot exist pre-conception, nor can he exist after death. "Joe is dead," is a nonsense sentence, but it is how our language has us think. Our language suggests that being dead can be a bad thing or a good thing. All of us would like being dead to be a good thing, somehow.

Death is the end of the process of dying. People can and always will do that. Once they have completed that process, there is nothing, at least as a state of being. A body exists. We call it Joe's body, but since Joe doesn't exist how can it be Joe's body? It *was* Joe's body, but it isn't Joe's body anymore. Joe existed from birth to the end of dying; before and after that, there ain't no Joe, there is nothing.

Death isn't nonlife; it's nothing, the same as before we were born. It may be useful to define dead as the instant at the end of life, but most people seem to think it is after that instant. The transition from life to nonlife is dying, and life is over when the dying is finished. I'm not even sure the word dying has much value except to announce that nonexistence is about to arrive from over the hill.

Being dead is not the end of all possibilities. It is not the end of life. Dying is the end of life. Dying is the end of all possibilities. Nor is dead a state of being or nonbeing.

Dead is a concept the same way my twin brother is a concept, and with equal reality. I don't have a twin brother. My twin never existed. Dead also doesn't exist. Life is real, with a beginning and an end; dead is a concept, a concept that has a beginning but no end (handy if one wants to imagine an eternal life).

For all of us, life is all there is. For survivors it is a different story; there is the reality of the dead body often mangled and needing disposal, the loss of potential, the loss of companionship, the empty space, the reality of never and the memories. Death exists only for those who remain.

Both my parents donated their bodies for medical research. The family received their cremated remains months after their deaths. My father was buried at Fort Rosecrans in San Diego, a beautiful hillside overlooking the bay and harbor. My mother joined him when she died.

I filled out the forms to donate my body to the University of Washington Medical School but haven't sent them in. I'm a body parts donor, but somehow can't yet get comfortable going all the way. I told my wife that I should be cremated with the remains pressed into a man-made diamond. I think this is a last-gasp effort at immortality. When I picture my ashes being tossed into the wind, I feel a distressing sense of finality and nothingness, but I'm comforted by the idea that a diamond is forever.

Until my friend ended her life, I was attracted to suicide as a means to control the uncertainties and helplessness of dying. While I was in graduate school, a private plane crashed in Lake Michigan killing the family on board except for the pilot, who was the husband and father. The plane had run out of gas. Pilot error. Within a year, the father killed himself, which I thought was a reasonable thing to do.

Ending one's life is fine, except for how it affects those who care about you. My friend Malcolm was in his early eighties and in hospice care when he decided that the quality of his days wasn't enough to warrant getting out of bed in the morning. One afternoon his wife drove to the local pharmacy with his death-with-dignity prescription, wrote a check and took home a pill that would kill her husband. He swallowed the pill at eleven-thirty one Tuesday morning and was dead by noon.

My wife and I had been invited to our friend's home the Sunday before, unaware of his decision. We chatted inanities for an hour or so and were leaving with a "see you later" when his sister broke the news as we walked to our car. I was hesitant to go back into the house to say a truly final goodbye; I had no idea how to do that, except to leave well enough alone—we're out of the house and half away, let's keep going, nothing we can do or say will make a difference. My wife said we had to go back. We went back. I clutched his hand in both of mine, looked him in the eye and said, "Thank you, Malcolm," and turned away. I don't know what my wife said.

While waiting in the car line for the return ferry, my wife and I shared our feelings. She experienced an extra layer of emotion because about fifteen years earlier she'd donated a kidney that had kept him alive. Now her healthy kidney would die with him, an odd awareness, I would think.

Malcolm was overbearing at times, but I learned at his memorial service that many people respected and benefited from him doing too much rather than too little. Yet he abandoned me when he could have postponed his dying for another week or two, enough for one more visit. I can't fathom what his wife was feeling as she fetched the death pill.

How does someone decide to die on a Tuesday at eleven-thirty in the morning? Was there a symbolic element I don't know about, or was it simply as convenient a time as any? What did he take into account in making his decision? Did he ask for an okay from his wife and sons? Did he imagine what it would be like to take the pill and wait to die? Did he care about last words? Was there any thought to making his end important in some way, as a coda to his life? As a humanist, my friend probably defined his end as just that, the stoppage of someone we knew as Malcolm and that was it. He wasn't gone; he just wasn't.

~ It Was All Robin's Fault ~

In *Personal Wisdom*, for which this memoir is a prequel, two metaphors were used to explain important elements of life; roots and the wind. Roots, such as culture and religion are the foundation of a person's life, giving stability, but also keeping you in one place. The wind is the ebb and flow of popular opinion, including the influences of friends. This chapter highlights the winds I faced over a few years, some minor, some major, some good, and some ill. The point is, the wind will blow and you have to deal with it. The chapter title is an inside joke. A few of us told our friend Robin that we would write a book "It Was All Robin's Fault." I'm glad I could give him at least a chapter here.

My first novel, *Invivo*, arose out of asking myself "what if?" after reading an article about Dolly, the cloned sheep. I was on an almost empty train between Glasgow and Edinburgh. As we rattled through the countryside, I could see plenty of sheep on the hills. Cloning didn't seem like such a big deal; all the sheep looked alike to me already. I understood the potential, though, and that got me thinking. Instead of replicating one set of DNA to produce identical sheep, *what if* you put one animal's DNA into the cells of a second animal? The cells would have twice the DNA to choose from during cell division.

Thus began the story of a Scottish researcher seeking the cure for genetic disease by doubling DNA in cells. Science, love, murder, revenge and justice in a rain-soaked Scottish glen.

What if, pointed at the future, can lead to unanticipated and life-expanding discoveries. Applied to the past, *what if* confirms that even hindsight is not twenty-twenty. What good is reflecting on the past? Does it bring clarity? Enable better future decisions? What if we never asked *what if*?

What if, along with its backward-viewing brothers and sisters, *if only, why didn't I*, and *I should have* (and cousins *if it wasn't for...* and *I coulda...*), are phrases that pretend that life is a game, complete with pause, repeat, reverse, undo and fast-forward buttons.

Let's play the *what if* game.

What if I had never met Robin? Instead of a relatively smooth ascendant life in sunny California, as I had planned, my career and life passage have been quite ragged. I've called almost thirty places home, three women "wife" and lost hundreds of thousands of dollars in business and personal finances; and it was all Robin's fault.

Robin was Robert Halley VII, who I met in graduate school. He was ahead of me by a little more than a year, already having a master's degree when I was taking my first classes. Robin was almost my height, sported a blond beard, spoke softly, demonstrated deep knowledge and a wide range of interests, and was the most warm, caring, gentle man I have ever known.

In spite of his natural empathic tendencies, we two combined into the major firepower of our intramural flag-football team, him throwing and me catching; the old and crafty graduate students squashing the younger, faster and stronger undergrads, unbeatable in our one glorious championship season.

Through graduate school we shared classes, hundreds of lunchroom debates in which he usually prevailed, dreams of our contributing to the benefit of humanity, feedback for one another's professional development and a passion for tennis and volleyball. He offered a thousand thoughtful opinions and I listened to all of them.

When I reminded Robin the state of my life was all his fault, he simply smiled a toothy grin from behind his beard. Everything he did was well meaning. I watched him once carry an ugly black spider cupped in his hands from the kitchen to the backyard. He thought he was being kind, not knowing then that indoor spiders don't do well outdoors.

Through a friend of Robin's, I met Jim, a navy physician who was separated from his wife. We first got together at his apartment where we chatted while lounging six inches off the floor in his beanbag chairs, knees as high as our heads, each with a glass of red wine which we set on the green shag carpet. I liked him immediately and told him that maybe we could become best friends.

We did. He and his estranged wife got back together and as couples, spent a lot of time together. Their friends became our friends. Here was a bag full of doctors and their wives, from all over the country, all intelligent and interesting, with great stories to share. Robin had created a social explosion for me.

Jim was interested in the human side of medicine, enough to establish what he called the men's group, meeting weekly for an hour or two to discuss the issues of being human, being a professional and being male. I was asked to facilitate, but during the first meeting the guys decided they didn't want a facilitator and invited me to become a member, which I did. I knew a lot about group process. Part of my training included participating in what were called encounter groups. We were supposed to tell the unvarnished truth to each other. During one, a fellow student said he didn't trust me. I was surprised; I couldn't understand why he would feel that way. I invited him into the middle of the group circle where we could discuss his comment in front of the others and he refused, leaving me to forever wonder what he meant. Another group experience conducted by an instructor was held in a remote room in a motel. I was lying on my back on a bare mattress on the floor. The instructor loomed over me and said, "Yes," while I was to say, "No," with matching intensity. We were soon shouting at each other. I was shaken by the force of emotion that could arise in such a simple exercise.

Groups can be harmful, but they can also be an effective way to understand and overcome personal issues. Esther

Globe ran a group at a clinic where early in my career I worked as the chief psychologist. I heard about her group and asked if I could cofacilitate. She agreed, knowing, I'm sure, that I wouldn't add much. She was a diminutive Jewish woman, an MSW rather than the newer LCSW, who wore tan support hose and sensible shoes that resembled thick ballet slippers. She was maybe in her late sixties. Most weeks, fifteen to twenty-five people would show up for her group, while the rest of us were lucky if three people attended ours. They sat in folding chairs in a tight circle, sometimes in rows two or three deep.

Eric Berne, who wrote *Games People Play* and invented Transactional Analysis (the three ego states of Parent, Adult and Child), wrote a book on group treatment, saying that it was easy to know if you were helping; you were helping if people continued to show up. Esther's people showed up every week and sometimes brought friends and neighbors for therapy. She played her group like conducting an orchestra. If Sally talked about her divorce, Esther would ask Harry, who was also going through one, what he heard. When Harry was done, she might ask if his statement about trying harder made sense to Tom who was looking for a job. In this way everyone was included, listening, being invited to contribute, or being told that they might want to think about what was being said. She was a maestro and her group loved her.

I watched in awe as she conducted her groups. She was an angel in frumpy clothes. Esther gave the people in her groups bite-sized pieces of their worlds they could chew and digest. She was able to ask the right question to focus someone's attention. She led them to draw conclusions and commit to doing something differently. I wondered how much she was clarifying and how much she might be manipulating. Just doing her job? A good soul helping the less fortunate? I wondered about the power of social pressure and group dynamics and joined another group myself.

The majority of the men's group members, and some guys who were not, made up another of my new friends' groups that would periodically go on a grovel: drinking and slumming as much as middle-class white guys would do who feared ruining their reputations. It was a well-meaning descent into decadence. Between four and maybe eight or nine guys would show up for dinner at an upscale place, usually downtown San Diego, La Jolla or maybe Hotel Circle. It would be a steak and martini place where we would order steaks and martinis and plan our entertainment for the evening. Being guys we tried to outdo one another in proposing increasingly debauched activities.

For my first grovel, the seven of us decided to go to one of the strip clubs off Rosecrans Avenue, the heart of the navy base area for after dark maneuvers. We strolled through the entrance of the club, turned a corner and entered a lobby, about the size of a two-car garage. It was empty except for us and a naked woman standing in the center of the room. She was maybe five feet and one inch, with short blonde hair, and was wearing nothing but high-heeled slippers and a friendly smile. When she raised her arm to point out the various entertainments I could see her side from armpit to ankle; somehow that made her more naked. Seven men, with shoes, socks, pants, shirts, even jackets and sweaters against the evening chill, and there was someone's little sister standing there naked. I was so surprised my mind flashed on the image of Botticelli's painting *The Birth of Venus*, and I'm not that cultured.

Later that night, over a fourth or fifth round of drinks, someone brought up exploitation. At first glance, that young woman was being exploited—ogled by packs of horny, drunk, probably obnoxious young men. Then again, she could have been making good money showing her body despite having few marketable skills and able to pay her tuition at junior college. We were the ones exploited. Want to see a naked girl? Twenty dollars, please. Want to touch? That will cost you more. Our biological drives made us vulnerable to long hair, a tight skirt and well-planned cleavage. Or that evening, to a naked lady.

We did this grovel thing maybe a half dozen times. Over the years, no one got a tattoo or did much of anything untoward. Dinner, a few drinks, a strip place maybe, but more often than not we went to a club and listened to music. I think we liked the idea of breaking loose, but went out together more for the company. Conversations almost always reverted to work and family. The end result for me? I was one of the boys. Life was great and getting better all the time, except for one shaky point.

My wife Rosemary and I had begun backpacking in the Sierra Mountains. During these trips she flowered. No longer being content to contribute from the background, she became a leader, a decision maker, someone willing and able to make tough calls. Until this time, she had been the woman I married, content to live in my shadow. Now she wanted to take weeklong treks without me.

I loved her and wanted her to be happy; it broke my heart that she wanted to find her happiness away from me.

When Rosemary eventually moved out to test the single waters, Jim was the first to offer support; his wife had recently ended their marriage. He listened as I tried to sort out how to make my marriage work until it was clear my wife had no intention of coming back. A few months after that realization, Jim and I were at my car after a guitar lesson when he asked, "Would you mind if I started dating Rosemary?" He hurriedly added that he wouldn't date her if I had any objections.

"Go ahead," I told him, and essentially dropped him from my social calendar. Which meant I had no friends from the men's group, the grovel group or his/my other friends. I also lost mutual friends who landed on my wife's side.

My wife left me, saying she needed to find herself. She loved me, I was a good husband, but out the door she went. What's the saying? "If you love something, set it free. If it comes back..." I wanted to support my wife.

My friend Jim said he wanted to date her. I wanted to support my friend. Interfering in her happiness and in his was not what I wanted to do. Want to this, want to that. I felt like crap, withdrew from the playing field and constructed an emotional isolation booth around myself.

It might have been sci-fi author Robert Heinlein who wrote about the Princess of the Seven Universes. From early childhood to early adulthood, she was primed to lead the vast federation of universes. One lesson she learned was that if she waited for a time, complex issues would disentangle themselves and she would be able to solve them. Thus I climbed into my isolation booth to wait it out.

As isolation booths go, mine was a honey, with lots of sunlight, bottles of gin and Scotch and a few bottles of red wine, a flow of pretty girls, a large TV and a great sound system. Dinners out during the week and golf on the weekends. I was respected at work and my patients improved. My life looked good. It wasn't a bad life. But it truly wasn't a good one. What I had loved, what I had wanted for my life had walked away.

The only friend I had left was Robin, the fellow who had started this particular ball rolling. He invited me to live with him for a while in his downtown La Jolla cottage, within walking distance of the village, the beach and the tennis courts. We enjoyed a bachelor's paradise, especially the tennis courts. Over perhaps the first four or five years of our friendship he never took a set off me in tennis, until one night when we were sharing his house he finally did; both of us felt the same emotions but in different proportions—relief, joy and contentment.

Robin helped me let go of Rosemary while his girlfriend set me up on a few dates. He found some professional opportunities for me. He also helped me cope with the death of one of my young patients in a motorcycle accident. Robin always wanted to help and I always wanted to listen.

In the span of about eighteen months the romance between Jim and my soon to be ex-wife cooled, Jim began making plans for his career after active duty, Robin got Jim and I reconnected, and Jim and I decided to create a practice together. Problems had untangled. Over the next few years we expanded, added docs and other staff, including one who became my second wife.

Jim and I have now been friends for almost forty years, my longest relationship with anyone. We have an uncanny ability to forgive one another, emphasize what we like about the other and accept each other's multitude of imperfections.

Robin and I had been friends for longer, but I lost him a couple of years ago to lung cancer. His wife Linda, along with his family and friends, said they would "love him to death," and they did. His golden beard was one of the casualties of his treatment. I'd never seen him beardless. When I visited during his last days, it was disconcerting to say good-bye to someone I didn't recognize.

It was all Robin's fault, because if I had not met him:

- My first wife and I would probably still be married and edging closer to our golden wedding anniversary.
- We might have had two or three children and quite possibly a dog.
- I would be semiretired but still working in my successful group psychology practice in Southern California.
- We'd be living in an ocean view home.
- I would be thirty pounds lighter and spending much of my free time playing golf and a bit of tennis at my country club.
- We would be middle-class affluent and I would be driving a Lexus.

But I did meet Robin and none of those things happened. It's Robin's fault, for without him Rosemary would not have had such an attractive option when she was exploring alternatives and became lonely and needy.

Without Robin I would probably have been part of a larger group practice of all psychologists. I would not have cashed in my life insurance policy to indulge a midlife crisis involving a low-slung, hot and throaty De Tamaso Pantera. I would not have suffered the pain of a second divorce.

Without Robin nudging the course of my life, I would have been living the one I originally intended.

To be fair, also because of the Robin effect:

- I am married to the love of my life.
- I worked with Jim and two other great guys for almost twenty years
- We lived in St. Andrews, Scotland, which was a grand adventure.
- I have stepchildren and grandchildren.
- I love leadership consulting and writing.
- I am as contented as a man can be.

Robin had a great professional and personal impact on my life. He suggested the life direction I decided to take. I learned a lot from him. I would sometimes put his name in the question, "What would _____ do?" For me he embodied a well-lived life. Partly because of Robin, I'm confident enough that I almost always put my own name in the blank space.

I was in my little isolation booth for about five years—thinking, pondering, lamenting, everything a person does to deal with getting punched in the face by life. Most of the five years were spent trying to make sense of what happened. Rosemary left me to find herself independent of any role such as daughter or wife. Jim was attracted to the same woman I found irresistible. Robin was doing his best to make connections for people he cared about. I was searching for the meaning of life. We were all doing the best we could. When I finally accepted that, I was ready to move on.

This is what I learned.

Rosemary ended our marriage in order to begin her own life. That's what she had to do. I clung to that missing marriage for five years from inside my isolation booth. My life had been wrenched away by the considered and conscious decision of someone else. But in those subsequent five years, I was throwing my own life away

Robin wasn't to blame for the misfortunes of my life as much as I liked to kid him that he was. If I had to blame anyone, heck, I'd blame Jim. But Jim wasn't to blame either, nor was it Rosemary, kismet, karma or any other form of fate.

"Things happen for a reason," is comforting, though unreasonable.

I decided to find a better way of coping with life events. My way is to live life as an ever-changing set of probabilities. Doing X increases or decreases the chances of Y. That's it, that's how life works. It's not Robin, Jim, God or Karma. It's my decisions, a trunk full of intended and unintended consequences, luck, mistakes, and everyone else's decisions. It's what I decide, whether in response to a naked lady, a yellow light at an intersection or how to live my life. It's a crowded world making it impossible to escape unscathed. It's up to me to be in charge as much as I can be, which is sometimes a lot and sometimes not at all.

As much as I would like it to be, my life isn't a story with a beginning, middle and end. My life is a collection of moments I am responsible for; I create the moment or I react to it. All I can do is my best, and accept that sometimes I'm not going to try hard enough, or I won't be good enough; and, as I have experienced, I will sometimes be beaten, hurt, damaged, disregarded and otherwise left feeling sorry I got out of bed that morning. People I love make mistakes and some of their decisions are not good for me. But I've made my share of mistakes and hurt people I care about too.

It's fair to wonder if making decisions based on the probability of a good personal outcome leads to self-recriminations when things go wrong. It doesn't. Sometimes results are bad, but how I got where I am is not. It seems like regretting an outcome puts attention at the wrong point; I can regret actions, not results.

Nobody wins the backward looking *what if* game. *What if* and all its past-focused iterations lead only to regrets. However, aimed at the future, *what if* identifies options and increases the chance of a good decision. Asking myself *what if* in the moment and sorting out the possibilities got me to where I am now, a good place. Reflecting on past *what if*s suggests an alternative life to the one I'm presently enjoying. If do-overs mean I'd end up someplace else, then no, there is no asking *what if*.

Thank goodness it wasn't Robin's fault. Nor was it my dad's, mom's, society's, the times or my circumstances growing up. I know that it's all my fault just like Jimmy Buffett in Margaritaville finally knew it was all his fault and accepting that, I can look in any kind of mirror and am content, even without a real beauty of a tattoo.

~ Self ~

Me. What about me? What is my responsibility to myself? Between birth and death is my time to do what I want—good, bad, indifferent, illegal, immoral and/or fattening. Since I am not burdened with overcoming original sin, or to meet the expectations of any religion or creed, I have a lot of free time, options and opportunity.

Currently there is an ad campaign on television that accurately describes my approach to myself. In the ads, a man asks four kids sitting around a table which is better; for example, "Is more better than less?" To one question, a boy said he made a New Year's "revolution." The man asked what it was and the boy replied, "Eat more jelly beans." That's my approach: eat more jelly beans.

I have two self-obligations: 1) to nurture myself so I can thrive, and 2) to reach for my ideal.

To thrive, I need to create as much intimacy with others as I possibly can. To touch and be touched; to have open and honest relationships with others to the greatest degree possible. Naturally, the closest relationships will be with family, but I have a few friends who are as close as any family members could ever be.

I also have to contribute value in order to thrive. It can be from small actions, like lighting the barbecue grill when my wife asks me to, or larger ones, such as a few weeks ago when I helped a group from King County, Washington, work together in a way many of them described as "life changing." That was great to hear. And I've been smart enough not to be rigid in how I thrive. I stopped playing volleyball a few years ago when I realized that I was no longer contributing to my team's success. I had become the weak link, a step or two slower than I used to be and no longer the guy who could be counted on to make the play. Something similar occurred with tennis. To get back into playing and to get back in shape as well, I joined a senior league when we lived on Whidbey Island. Turns out most of the old guys were playing geezer tennis. In this form of tennis, the player hits a drop shot at the first opportunity and when the opponent races to the net to get it, he then hits a lob deep in the court that the opponent has to run back and get. The geezer would then hit another drop shot and so on. He would keep up this style of play until the opponent dropped from exhaustion. It wasn't fun and didn't add to my nurturing myself. After encountering three straight opponents with this type of game, I took myself out of play.

Thriving means continually finding new ways of enjoying life as the old ones fail to work. For me, reaching for my ideal is a part of thriving when I get out of bed. What I mean by ideal is being able to do old things better and learn how to do new things. I read probably three to five hours a day—the newspaper, magazines, and usually I'm somewhere into three or four books. I'm constantly redoing presentations and training outlines. I'm lucky to have colleagues who teach me something every time I'm with them. And, of course, my wife is able to discover minor flaws that could use a bit of polishing. I think she is mildly afraid of my inevitable decline suddenly accelerating, so she keeps watch and offers suggestions.

I know my mind isn't working as well as it used to; nor is my body. It's amusing, actually, to watch myself go through what my parents did, what aunts and uncles did, what my older friends did and are doing. So-called liver spots cover my hands and arms. My former beautiful biceps, like knotted ropes just months ago, are now as smooth as a fashion model's. My night vision while driving is not so sharp. I do my best to avoid the old person syndrome of talking too much or offering unsolicited opinions and am especially wary of the middle-aged male tendency to tell lame jokes to amuse women. While watching television with my wife, I try not to point to the TV and ask, "Is that guy dead?" I also try not to say "I used to." Who cares what I used to do? I don't even care. It's what I do now that counts. Thrive and grow. Thrive and grow.

Bottom line? I am fine as I am. I'm not the smartest, the best-looking, the most charming, the nicest, the most anything, yet this is my life, and I'm all I've got. I can't be anything more than I am.

There are two elements to self-acceptance for me: 1) it is folly to compare myself to any of the other seven billion-plus humans in the world, and 2) as long as I'm growing, I'm doing okay. And by growing, it's how I want to grow, not another person's idea. It doesn't have to be much and it doesn't have to be often, but it has to be what's best for me. Movement is life; movement in what I think is the right direction is a life worth living.

~ The Meaning of Life ~

It is mid-year, 2015. Gays have full marriage rights in the United States, Queen Elizabeth is the longest reigning monarch in British history, genome sequencing becomes common medical treatment, the Carteret Islands are abandoned due to global warming, while in Seattle, the minimum wage is fifteen dollars an hour. And for me, at the age of sixty-nine years and two months, I am close enough to the end of my life to arrive at some confident conclusions. I know what the meaning of life is. At least I know what it is for me. Of course, that's all that matters. I am the center of the universe. My hope is that my conclusions will be of benefit to you as you construct and explore your universe.

Life includes terrorists who believe that blowing up other people pleases God. It includes men who enjoy fondling little girls and boys. In many places, parents struggle to find enough food to feed their children and sadly, countless thousands of these same children die of dehydration or other easily treated ailments. Billions of dollars are spent on war machines when eleven dollars each could give sight to thirty million of the blind. We are a powerful yet immature species and deserve to become extinct before we ruin the planet for every other living thing.

Before we destroy the earth, and ourselves we have the chance, each of us, to figure out what to do with this gift of life.

I decided long ago that my life should have a purpose and I had to figure out that purpose. Although my final decision might be the same as many others, it would have been a mistake to borrow what worked for them, like a religion or moral code. There is an old Irish proverb: "You have to do your own growing no matter how tall your grandfather was." Without knowing that I had decided for myself, I would never be sure I was living my life rather than a life designed for someone else.

This created a challenge. I had to examine everything, potentially dismissing the critical wisdom and insights of others to judge from my own extremely limited perspective. Who was I to suspect and even disregard the centuries-old values of millions of people smarter and more experienced than I? What was answer enough for me was: They are not me and I am not them. I would make mistakes, sure, and I would waste time wandering the corridors of questions and uncertainty, searching for a door to go through that made sense to me. But what else was my life for?

The answer to that is in two parts. First, my life is for me. That's it. My life is for me and I want to live it the best way I can find. Rabbi Hillel once said, "If I cannot be for myself, who can I be for?" and I took that idea to heart. The meaning of life just for me is to touch and be touched; to create an intimacy with others so great that love is the most precious life experience and lost love is almost unbearably painful.

Second, the meaning of life had to include something bigger than just my life. Hillel also said, "If I am only for myself, what kind of man can I be?"

Early during the search, the meaning of life was the search itself. Frankly, that wasn't fulfilling. It felt like I was just hoping I was living a good life. I did the small things I knew were important, supporting the usual good causes like a clean environment and similar efforts to do what I thought was right. But there wasn't the confidence that I was doing the best I could. There wasn't a code or catechism I could follow to know I was on the right course. Without the luxury of following a well-worn path, I was stuck beating back a jungle of options. The alternative was to accept one of the more common routes, like being a good Catholic or Republican or whatever.

Rejecting religion was tough at first. People a lot smarter than I were staunch believers. I didn't have the brainpower to trust I was right and they were wrong. But at the same time, having a God create and run the world didn't make sense. For me there were too many unacceptable elements that drove me away.

Religion began in primitive times when people were trying to understand the seasons, fire, the movement of water, light and dark, birth and death... basically everything. It was comforting to invent spirits that controlled nature's mysteries, for otherwise they would be happening without cause. Over time, this construction became more organized, spirits were named and relationships formed between spirits and man.

There is also the question of why any all-powerful deity would bother creating heaven and earth. I would think any self-respecting God would have more important things to do than create a set of toys to lord over. And a super-being demanding to be worshiped? Worshiped by his creations? How does that make sense? Instead of his creations wasting time repeating rituals, you would think a rational God would want people to explore their individuality, their commonalities, the wonders of the world and the unlimited boundaries of imagination; the essence of the gift they were given.

I get a kick out of a football player praising God for helping him score a winning touchdown. People who thank God for saving them in a flood are interesting too. Who do they believe is responsible for the flood that put them in danger in the first place?

God is a wonderful idea that provides comfort in the direst circumstances and for that reason alone has great value. Those who live according to the true values of religion lose nothing if they are wrong and in the meantime help create a world worth living in. I like the idea of

God in part because I'd love to be there as those who bastardize God's word arrive at the Pearly Gates and with significant horror realize they are going to hell. Sadly, that won't happen. Those bastards will end up like the rest of us.

My friend J. Corbett taught me that if you believe in God, you then have purpose and can work toward creating your particular brand's meaning of life. The rest of us, he said, have to find meaning *in* life. That's a profound difference, *of* and *in*. *Of life* means that the beginning, middle and end are important. *In life* means only the middle is important. That's where I live.

So for us poor bastards who don't have everlasting life to look forward to, what's the point of living? Why not exist in a haze of illicit drugs until we slide unaware into a fatal overdose? With no purpose other than what we make up, why not be as oblivious of life's pain as we can be?

Answering that question was one reason why the search for meaning was a useful exercise; it kept me busy until something better came along. Without that search, it was possible that I could have chosen to pass my days in an alcohol-fueled fog.

However, choosing a self-induced oblivion would have diluted the existential angst that initially fueled my search for meaning. A addled view of myself and the world meant that I might as well be dead already, ending all options; this was not an acceptable state to be in, at least while I still cared about getting out of bed in the morning.

With searching for meaning, at worst I'd be like Thomas Edison finding ten thousand ways not to construct a light bulb, and at best I'd uncover my life's mission.

About ten years ago I discovered the meaning of life. One day I was pondering and suddenly all the thinking, reading, talking and listening meshed. People have needs. If the first part of the meaning of life is about me, the second part of the meaning of life is to help others meet their needs: And not just people, all living things. The meaning of life is so simple I can describe it in one word, contribute. That's it: contribute. This is the essence I had been searching for. Not earth shattering, I know. You could ask a hundred people what the meaning of life is and many would say the same thing. I had been seeking the answer for forty years by that point, seeking something grand, profound, monumental, something worth climbing a mountain to learn. Then I realized that it couldn't be monumental. I'm not monumental and the meaning of life had to fit me. Most people aren't monumental, so how could the meaning of life be monumental? It has to fit each of us, no matter who or what we are.

Everyone who recognizes the potential of being alive derives a sense of meaning from contributing and each does it in his or her own way, giving to God, family, and/or fellow man. Boy Scouts learn the meaning of life when they are taught to leave a campsite cleaner than when they arrived. Golfers have the concept of repairing the small pit their ball makes when it hits the green, plus one more that another player failed to fix. An important component of life's meaning is to know you have a choice and to make one. Mindlessly following a creed or social norm isn't enough. It's like wearing a hat. If you wear a hat because everyone around is wearing a hat, there is no real awareness of options. There is no meaning in automatically following everyone else. ("Only a dead fish always goes with the flow.") You may be living an exemplary life, but without a deliberate choice, you are devaluing your unique point of view. Meaning first comes from knowing about choice and then from the choice you make.

Put yourself in the role of the soldier who shot the pilot. What was going on in his mind? Did he get out of bed that morning with the intent of shooting someone? Did he hate the enemy? Did he enjoy what he was doing? Did he feel he had to follow orders? Did he know he had a choice? Making a choice for yourself is important; deciding how to contribute to others is significant.

Parents are especially vulnerable to tough choices. A little girl who lived nearby spent half her life in the hospital or at home recovering. Only infrequently was she able to attend school. She died before her sixth birthday. Her parents were aware of the impossible odds of survival when she was diagnosed with neuroblastoma, but they could not give up hope in spite of her suffering. While she was alive, they had to make the choice to try one more invasive test, one more painful treatment.

After her death, they had to make the choice of how to continue their own lives. (Few marriages withstand this trauma.) Collectively, the glory of humankind is in the struggle. Individually, the struggle is why we must have meaning greater than our personal lives.

A former colleague of mine often gives speeches. His favorite story is of meeting another bike rider on one of his cross-country trips. This biker rode long distances, a thousand miles or more each time. My coworker asked him what he remembered best about these trips. The biker said, "The hills, I remember the hills," and described both the effort required and the feeling of conquering the challenges.

Meaning in life relies on having hills to climb. That's the easy part; there are enough hills in all our lives. Coping with these hills demands a sense of a bigger picture, a reason to make the effort. This is where meaning in life causes conflict. When contributing to others, whose point of view must be considered? People see the big picture differently. One difficulty is that people with power and a different definition of meaning can force you to do it their way.

For example, legislators vote on a wide range of significant issues such as abortion or the death penalty or funding for the homeless. Often, these decisions are made along party lines. A political philosophy drives how votes are cast and meaning is defined.

A national politician is strongly opposed to gay marriage until his daughter wants to marry another girl; then everything changes. These lawmakers operate from unexamined, self-absorbed points of view, without the requisite experience or wisdom to make a truly informed decision for all constituents. As I realized at seventeen, politicians have no secret store of wisdom.

Rheba de Tornyay was the power behind the University of Washington's rise to become the number one nursing school in the country. She was outspoken and tough; people listened to and acted on her opinions. She was against doctor-assisted suicide and against medical marijuana… until she became ill with cancer. Her pain was successfully diminished with marijuana and her death, "private," was a relief.

These people are the leaders who sway public opinion, who make the laws that govern everyone's rights and freedoms. Why can't individuals legally end their painful last days and why should anyone have the power to say they can't? Often those who deny such freedoms do so because of religious beliefs. Spreading God's love is of inestimable value; people spreading His judgment, not so much.

Texas, the state that executes more criminals than any other, currently and ironically is keeping alive a dead woman. Thirty-three-year-old Marlise Munoz was brain-dead after collapsing in her kitchen from a blood clot in her lung. She was fourteen weeks pregnant at the time of her death. Texas law prohibits shutting off vegetative support in such cases. Munoz's mother said, "It's not a matter of pro-choice and pro-life. It's about a matter of our daughter's wishes not being honored by the state of Texas." Both mom and the fetus were without oxygen for more than an hour after her collapse. But the fetus has a heartbeat. The father, Ernest Machado, said, "All she is, is a host for a fetus. I get angry with the state… Why are they practicing medicine up in Austin?"

Also in the great state of Texas, the Republican Party practiced psychotherapy by ratifying their platform in mid-2014 to include "reparative therapy" for gays (gays who seek "healing and wholeness [by moving away] from their homosexual lifestyle"), thus ensuring support of traditional family values and the protection of marriage being between one man and one woman.

Legislators who are religious should have to document why and how their belief is in the public interest as a whole. Those who do not buy into the fables must not be held hostage by those who do. Belief is a wonderful state of being… for those who believe. Others must not be affected, limited or subjected.

Bertrand Russell put it well:

> The whole problem with the world is that fools and fanatics are always so certain of themselves, but wiser people so full of doubts.

Doubt is the engine that drives fruitful discussion.

Fruitful discussion is the path that makes the world a better place for everyone. Thus my struggle with uncertainty and trying to learn from everyone was the most effective route for me to understand what was truly important: living the right life for me and not living the life of someone else and, equally importantly, contributing to, not interfering in, other people's lives.

I understand that those in power are faced with decisions that cannot equally benefit everyone and I understand that politicians have to keep their message simple while appealing to enough people to win the election and stay in office. One of the dilemmas of democracy is that those in power have more information about the state of things than the voters who must choose them. Another problem is that the support of free speech translates to political groups fabricating whatever makes opponents look bad. What I ask of those who seek or are in power might be difficult, but here it is. Politicians, religious leaders, bosses, even bloggers must take care to balance their positions with support for those with other views. This could entail defining their platform, then listing both the pros and cons of their position. What delightfully disruptive innovation that would be. We should commit to uncertainty (and consequently to the truth).

After fifty years of searching for the meaning of life, what fascinates me is that what you choose doesn't matter. As long as you ask the right questions and the answers feel right to you, you're finding what you're looking for. You must parse life into small enough parts so you know what you are doing. Too large a view assumes that global concepts rule everyone, the end justifies the means, and everyone is essentially the same. Too small a view without a guiding vision puts us into a what's-in-it-for-me mode. In between are individuals who must decide what to do with their days, the needs of others and moral questions. Many have said this before me: do what you think is best and continuously question what you do. (Walt Whitman put it this way: "Re-examine all that you have been told... dismiss that which insults your soul.")

The general course of my life is guided by only three questions, two to be answered in the affirmative and the other in the negative:

> Is it right for me?

> Does it contribute?

> Does it hurt anyone else?

I aspire to answering these three questions with three affirmatives:

> Is it right for me?

> Does it contribute?

> Does it uphold everyone else?

Then I know my life has meaning. Personal wisdom is the method, living my life well is the result.

DETRITUS

~ Detritus ~

My mechanical incompetence aside, two of my high school years included being an audio-visual technician. During free periods, my responsibility was to wheel movie and slide projectors to and from classrooms and, behind the scenes, splice broken film.

I took great pride in splicing films so well that there was no jump when the film ran through the projector sprockets. Lining up the tiny holes was critical. Also, I made sure there was little film lost to the cutting room floor. The secret was to find the part of the film in the best condition for a splice, but at the point closest to where the film needed repair.

The same approach applied to this book. I did my best to include only what was necessary to tell the story and lined everything up to read smoothly. What was left over, but still valuable, is in this section. Life is comprised of moments, some attached together in long strings, some isolated. The following are isolated thoughts, observations and the like that added to my learning the meaning of life.

My father asked me one time what he could have done better as a father. I made the mistake of telling him; but to his credit I believe he eventually forgave me.

There may be serious things wrong with me. I don't have any heroes and I believe patriotism has caused more harm than good. And it is better to live for your country than to die for it.

A few years ago my first wife got word that I had died. When I heard about that, it felt weird, but strangely comforting.

Attending writers' conferences has taught me that the primary goal of a good writer is to tell the truth. At times I believe there is no truth; other times I realize I don't know the truth, although there is probably truth somewhere. At the moment I think truth is agape love.

Aha moments are those times of insight when you finally understand what you thought you already knew—if you don't have at least a minor one fairly frequently, you're not doing it right. Delightful surprise is one of the rewards of being uncertain.

I chose not to father children, feeling that it was not my right to bring someone into life without being able to ensure that life would prove to be a good experience. I missed a lot, but the decision still feels like the right one. I don't think they mind.

My stepchildren have been as fulfilling as any children could be and the grandchildren, oh my, all I can say is, I had no idea.

There is no better life experience than when a child gleefully runs to you.

About nine-tenths of the time I truly understand women and very much admire what I understand.

I would vote for any politician whose platform included ending all telephone solicitations, creating a flat tax, and passing a law that only a small percentage of lawmakers can be lawyers; the majority would have to be social workers, business people and teachers, and their overall demographics must reflect those of the areas governed.

And another thing: campaign donors should be able to donate only to candidates they're eligible to vote for; taxes should be on wealth as well as income; and companies are not people, so they cannot vote, which means they shouldn't be able to contribute to political campaigns.

For a presentation one time I made up the story that my mother once told me, "If you can say something nice to someone, do it." She would have said this if she had thought of it. I try to follow her advice.

I learned a lesson this week that might finally stick; it was a five-part lesson. It began Wednesday when I was driving home from a short business trip, cruising along in the third freeway lane behind a car going my speed, seventy miles per hour. I noticed a mile ahead that a line was forming in the fourth lane due to a backup on the exit ramp. The car in front of me slowed, just as I would in case someone decided to pull out of the line. As we approached the backup, he slowed more, down to forty then thirty; he was a smart, cautious driver. Then he drove slower yet. The guy ahead of me wasn't being safe; he ignored the end of the line and was now trying to cut in. We slowed to ten then five. Cars whizzed by in the next lane, I was stuck crawling along as he looked for someone he could cut off. He found his victim and finally got out of my way. I punched the gas and hit the horn at the same time.

I instantly regretted doing so. He could have pulled out, chased me down, cut me off and punched my face in. Or he could have followed me, as menacing as the dorsal fin of a shark moving along the shoreline. Neither happened and I wasn't worried they would. No, my remorse was in response to yet another of my kneejerk reactions to a personal slight—and I mean slight; I take huge personal offense at the least provocation. I do this kind of thing two or three times a year and always wonder why I am so small-minded. I again told myself to change.

Part two of the lesson occurred two days later at a wedding. I met a guy named Steve who was writing a book based on scripture that detailed God's plan, including seven states of being after death. The varied states included hell. I mentioned to Steve that any God that sought vengeance seemed to have suspect godliness. What kind of god would need such a thing? He had a pat answer that avoided the issue, so I remained of the opinion that vengeance was a sin no matter who sought it.

This second lesson had its delayed impact during lesson three, the next day. My wife and I were having breakfast at a nearby diner, The Sugar Shack, a dive place with red booths, Formica tables and old rock 'n' roll posters on every wall. Over waffles I brought up suing the woman who earlier in the year had hit my wife's car.

My wife had been at a red light in the left turn lane when she was rammed from behind, causing thirty-five hundred dollars of damage. The woman refused to cooperate with our insurance company so we were out our five hundred dollar deductible. I wanted to sue her in small claims court, but my wife said no, that the other woman was struggling. I then realized my intent was vengeance, just like God's.

Part four of the lesson occurred at 3:25 this morning. One of our two cats, Rocket del Fuego Brown, likes to sleep in the crook of my legs. When I move, he waits patiently until I'm settled again then returns to his favorite spot. He doesn't bite or claw me, doesn't meow his displeasure, he simply accepts what I'm doing and adapts.

The fifth and final portion of my lesson was a memory of my granddaughter Caitlin when she was three and a half. Her soccer class was running amok with ten rug rats and ten balls in a pint-sized jitterbug of running kids, flailing legs and bounding soccer balls. Suddenly Caitlin was blindsided, knocked down by another little girl. The look on her tiny face was shock, pain, even sadness that her world was suddenly a hurtful place.

I had noticed that other kids who were knocked down got up crying and waited until a parent arrived to comfort them. Caitlin got up and I could sense her mental wheels turning: my world was just violated, how am I going to react? I choose to believe she decided to ignore the assault and return to playing soccer. Which is what she did; I don't know why.

My error is to put a personal slight on the same continuum as a Japanese soldier bayoneting a bound civilian rolling down a hill. My brain defines the situation as: this is unacceptable. And then I blame someone. Better people than I say to themselves: a bad thing happened and I must figure out how to fix it or adjust to it.

Five lessons courtesy of a jerk driver, a man of God (or maybe God himself in disguise), another errant driver (and my wife), a cat and a granddaughter. Soon, in the last gasp of my sixties, I hope to finally reach the level of a mature three-and-a-half-year-old.

While working with a group of social workers on leadership, I learned that most health care workers and other caretakers don't consider themselves leaders. So I defined leadership as helping others succeed. Most then decided they were indeed leaders and began making an effort to improve how they led.

When I was first married, my wife and I were adopted by a stray cat—a jet-black, straggly little kitten. I had an allergy but we decided to keep him anyway. He was great, playing fetch with a ball of yarn and ceaselessly bounding in seemingly random directions. His high energy quickly vanished, though, and we took him to a vet—an unaffordable expense for us at the time. After the exam, the doctor recited a long list of ailments and then was silent. My wife, who grew up with cats, started crying. Evidently, this was the start of a difficult conversation I knew nothing about. We ended up choosing option B, spending only the money necessary to humanely kill the cat. I thought then, and still think today, that it would be ironic symmetry to have my own life end due to insufficient funds for needed medical care. And it may happen, given the current health care battles in the US.

Most women get it, most men don't; no matter what "it" is. Women prove that to me every day.

One of my favorite quotes is from Robert Frost:

> Don't ever take down a fence until you
> know why it was put up.

Small things can mean a lot. I remember when I was sixteen and desperate for a driver's license. So desperate I got up at five a.m. during summer vacation to take a driver's education class from six until nine. Finally the day came when I could take the test. I passed. Within minutes of arriving home, I asked my parents if I could drive the family car to my friend Pete's house. My dad tossed me the keys and I was soon on the streets of my neighborhood, driving by myself. It was a small gesture of trust from my parents but I remember it with fondness today, more than fifty years later. I don't know if they were worried for me, for the car, or if they didn't have any anxiety after having gone through a similar experience when my older sister began driving. It doesn't matter. It was a small gesture and it meant a lot to me.

This is book number fifteen for me. My books may be my form of life after death. I hope they'll be around a while so I can make a lasting contribution. If my books are available past the time my family has directly known me, maybe three generations, that's plenty long enough.

Grandchildren are life's most enriching invention; they make me feel old and wise and youthful at the same time.

Currently I think the best song in the world is "Somewhere Over the Rainbow," the version by Israel (Iz) Kamakawiwo'ole. A very close second is Bobby Darin's "A Simple Song of Freedom."

Compared to all other human beings who ever lived, the quality of my life has to be in the top 0.0000001 percent. That is both hugely lucky and hugely motivating. After all, I could have been born a cockroach and been a friend to no one.

For me, my dad provided direction while my mother provided support. Their overlapping division of responsibility worked well.

I haven't yet figured out the value of symbols. Wearing a uniform or sporting a certain pin enables people to feel like members of a group. That's fine. But what about giving up your life to safeguard something like your nation's flag? Or killing your child because he or she has somehow dishonored the family name? Is there a clear dividing line between symbol and reality I don't know about that makes sense of this kind of stuff?

One of my favorite ways of feeling connected to human-kind is to explore who was alive during my lifetime (like Orville Wright who died two years after I was born, thus connecting me directly with the birth of flight), and who was alive during my parents' and grandparents' lifetimes. I also count the least number of people's lives (I use life spans of ninety years) that connect me to important historical events like Columbus sailing the ocean blue or the invention of the printing press. Less than a thousand lives connect me to early man first wandering out of Africa into the rest of the world. It takes only three people to connect me to the American Revolution and twenty-two to the birth of Christ. My connection with the executed pilot is much closer; he was probably killed after my sister was born.

One of my favorite activities at dinner parties is to ask: if we could suspend the laws of time and space, what event would you like to observe or what person would you like to meet? My first idea was to sit in a lawn chair with a glass of iced tea and observe the big bang in slow motion, with Albert Einstein sipping his drink next to me explaining what was happening, especially the five minutes prior to the big bang (in order to see what nothing looked like). The second time we did it, I wanted to see my parents at play when they were preteens in Glasgow. I was curious to see what they were like and what they did as kids.

Another difference between men and women I've noticed is that women actually go looking for things that need to be cleaned.

The best moment of my life occurred when I realized I was in love with the woman who would become my current and hopefully last wife. We were an hour into our first date, dinner at her house, when we bantered about a dollar bet. It was a lightning bolt, thunder, roller coaster, wide-eyed wonder and intravenous amphetamine all at once. As I mentioned earlier I was so stunned by the experience that I didn't call her for a week after our date, almost ruining the best moment that would ever grace my life.

Maybe because I'm Scottish, I tend to be tight with a dollar. What I have learned, but not yet well enough, is that by seeking the cheapest, I lose the benefit of having the best. I do a lot for myself like designing my websites. (I'm pleased with www.collwisdom.com) I enjoy figuring out how to do new things, but with such talent that abounds in the world, I miss the pleasure and benefit of high quality work done by people who know what they're doing. These people can create art where I jury-rig something barely good enough. I have never regretted paying for quality, but still have trouble opening my wallet.

We were playing tackle football during second grade recess. I grabbed my classmate Warren. At that age, when a kid is grabbed he goes down, collapsing as if shot in one of our cowboys and Indians games. Warren didn't. He wiggled his hips and moved his legs as if dancing the Charleston, refusing to go down. I could have been kicked in the face. I was so surprised I let go and off he went. It took a while for me to realize that we boys cooperated with one another to play *at* football. We went down when tackled because we were supposed to, not because of the force of the tackle. We didn't care who won or lost; we played for fun. Warren was the first to actually compete. Now there were winners and losers. Much of my naivety is due to not yet understanding in this world of ours when to cooperate and when to compete.

While in the military I decided that I would never work for someone who was dumber than I am. Whenever I ignored that rule, I paid the price.

I understand the motivation of terrorists. They can't succeed against six hundred billion dollar annual military budgets and rocket-equipped drones so they have to attack crowded marketplaces, marriage ceremonies and funerals to have any chance of making a point, let alone prevailing. The concept is that the end justifies the means. What they fail to realize is that it is a rare end that can justify the means. Most of what we have is an endless series of means. That's true for them; that's true for all of us. What we do now is how the world works; that's it. Our ultimate goal means nothing; it's all in what we do along the way.

I've worked for a few companies that emphasized creating the right image. I don't even know who I am well enough, let alone know how to create the right image of me. These jobs never worked out, which was good all around. It's comforting to suppose that people who don't have much of an identity are better at creating the right image.

Every once in a while I like to ponder the idea of infinite space, or at least, the idea of an expanding universe. I can't conceptualize what is on the other side of the edge of the universe and I really don't fully understand the balloon analogy or the inflation concept. But my body takes up space and it's intriguing to think about my tiny portion of space in comparison with planets and stars and galaxies. Which element of the universe has the most significance? I think the answer is delightful. Little old me; I have more significance than anything else in the cosmos. Except for you.

I kicked one of our two cats late last night. I was walking down our hallway in the dark and the cat was coming the other way. I didn't see it and I hit the cat with my foot full on, mid-stride in its stomach. The cat immediately raced to the garage and wouldn't come out. I had just finished effective consulting work that day and was feeling great. Until I kicked the cat.

Sometimes when I look at the palms of my hands, they remind me of my father's. When I rub them slowly together, they feel like my dad's hands felt.

My body knows more about life than I do. It tells me when I have to pee. My body successfully fights off infections before I know I have one. My heart beats 630,000 times a week whether I ask it to or not. This is bothersome. I thought I was in control. I don't want hair growing out of my ears.

As I see it, morals have developed in this way:

No morals	Behavior is instinctual
Seed of morals	Don't harm kin
	Support kin
Basic morals	Don't hurt those who are different
Advanced morals	Support everyone

Humanity operates between the seed of morals and basic morals. If there is a lesson here, I suppose it's that everyone should find his or her own way, and do it at a higher moral code than humanity as a whole has been able to reach. That's sounds like a meaningful life to me.

Religious folks who hear evolutionists saying we descended from monkeys often conclude that nonbelievers are suggesting that God looks like a monkey. Besides applying bad logic, they miss a grand opportunity. Could anyone believe that I am in God's image, a six-foot male with toenails that need clipping and hairy armpits? Am I like God with a bit of extra suet around the middle or is He more like our ideal with six-pack abs? How absurd. We are not the physical manifestation of God. God isn't physical. Man can be in God's image in the wondrous and infinite potential of life itself—hope, creativity, love and compassion. If believers were not so worried about defending past definitions, they could embrace all of the grand possibilities.

Years ago, as a director in a moderate-sized company, I made a mistake. It didn't cost the company anything and no one was hurt. I even forget what the mistake was. When my boss talked to me about it, she said she wouldn't punish me because she knew I would punish myself enough about it. That didn't make sense to me. Why should an adult be punished for making an honest mistake? We all make them; we don't intend to make them but we do. How does punishment improve the situation? The Just Culture folks have it right, but I wonder how much impact their approach has.

Three of my friends suffer from White Hat Syndrome— a mostly male affliction suffered by those who believe they are always right. Trouble is, for the most part, they are right about always being right. They are very smart and have proved to themselves that the way they see something is most often the best way. They feel little compulsion offering opinions, suggestions, thoughts, reflections and so on, no matter what the topic. I used to resent it, until I learned of their good intentions. The sufferers of this malady do suffer, when they are rejected by the likes of me for only trying to help.

I used to think capital punishment was wrong, until I thought about the family and friends of the victim. If they needed the death of the bad guy in order to move on, so be it. Then it occurred to me that this was too much like vengeance, a bad reason to do anything.

Killing someone is wrong no matter who does it and with what kind of system safeguards. As for war, killing an enemy combatant is unfortunately the right of sovereign states, no matter how wrong it is.

In the early version of my book *Personal Wisdom*, I introduced the idea of becoming perfect. I tried for fifteen years to sell the concept but nobody liked it. See if you do. The idea is that if you do these three things, you will be perfect:

1. Care about yourself and others.
2. Admit to mistakes and fix them as well as you can.
3. Pursue personally meaningful goals.

What do you think? Is the perfect life possible and is this the way to achieve it?

For quite a while I was attracted to the Buddhist concept of ridding oneself of all human needs and desires, basically becoming empty, in order to reach enlightenment. Then it occurred to me that this state of being empty was essentially being dead. Why eliminate the essence of yourself before actually dying? My idea is to embrace what it means to be human, the unique human that is you. Find enlightenment through the expression and exaltation of who you are, all the good, bad, wonderful and messed up stuff that is you.

What has to be one of my top ten lessons of life is realizing that people who are different from me should not be feared or challenged, but embraced as wonderful opportunities for exploring new universes.

After reading a magazine article, I often find myself agreeing with the author, until I read the follow-up letters to the editor. I'm surprised how often I agree with the letter writer too. Such letters make me more confused and uncertain, and I think, wiser.

My most profound personal moment occurred one clear night on Whidbey Island. We were living in what we called the Bluff House, on the western shore of the island where in some directions our nearest neighbors were twenty-five miles away. I set up the telescope my wife gave me for my birthday, found Jupiter and focused on two of its moons. That moment of clearly seeing the two moons against the massive planet five-hundred million miles away somehow put *me* into perspective.

When my older granddaughter was three, I told her that everyone in the family had jobs. The number of jobs was the same as how old they were. I asked her how old she was and when she said, "three," I said she had three jobs. She liked the idea, but wasn't totally sure. Job number one, I told her, was to play. She liked that. I said that job number two was to learn things. She liked that job too.

Job number three was to be safe. I could see she was disappointed in that one. Then I said, "You know what, that's one of my jobs too, to keep you safe. We have the same job!" That was great. She reaches for my hand when we walk in parking lots so we can do our jobs together.

The reason I included the above vignette is that I'm more an observer than a participant. Those that lead the charge, make the big play and take the big chance are far ahead of the likes of me who prefer to reflect and understand. I give children a new idea, I don't fight for freedoms. There is a continuum of life experience that I seemed to appreciate from very early on. I was lucky to find what worked for me.

A practical definition of *contribute* is: pick something outside of yourself and make it better.

OTHER INFLUENCES AND INSPIRATIONS

~ Books and Other Writings/Audio ~

I have learned more about life and people reading novels and popular nonfiction than I did studying psychology texts. Perhaps books that I read for enjoyment spoke to me in ways I could hear more clearly.

How to Live: Or A Life of Montaigne in One Question and Twenty Attempts at an Answer, Sarah Bakewell

A solid introduction to Montaigne's thinking— well written and engaging.

"Great Minds of the Eastern Intellectual Tradition," Grant Hardy, The Great Courses, DVD

Professor Hardy is a geeky, personable presenter in this set of lectures of the great minds and religions I knew little about.

I and Thou, Martin Buber

Started me thinking about you, me and God.

Personal Knowledge: Towards a Post-Critical Philosophy, Michael Polanyi

He put the person in the middle of knowledge; I used his title idea for my book on *Personal Wisdom*.

The Origin of Consciousness in the Breakdown of the Bicameral Mind, Julian Jaynes

Fascinating study of how our ancient brain talked to itself and how that evolved into personal awareness.

Educational System Planning, Roger A. Kaufman

Helped me understand how to create a process for people to learn. One of my favorite graduate school professors.

The Creators: A History of Heroes of the Imagination, Daniel J. Boorstin	Inspirational story after inspirational story about the most fascinating minds.
Shōgun, James Clavell	Read on a rainy backpacking trip in the Sierra Mountains. Helped me understand the brutality of the Japanese culture.
Hawaii, James A. Michener	Another most enjoyable way of understanding people, family and duty.
Slaughterhouse-Five, Kurt Vonnegut	Helps put the absurdity of war into perspective.
The Old Man and the Sea, Ernest Hemingway	I wanted to be like the old man and to write like Hemingway.
The Good Earth, Pearl S. Buck	Deepened my understanding of life and death and the dignity of life.
What is Thought? Eric B. Baum	Finally had a clear idea of how my mind worked.
Guns, Germs, and Steel, Jared Diamond	And had a better idea how societies work and evolve.
The Story of Civilization, Will and Ariel Durant	Reading this series had a profound effect on my understanding of the world, especially religion and how people can have profound impact good and bad.

Great Books of the Western World, University of Chicago and the "Harvard Classics"	Saved me when I was in the military. I could listen to the great minds of the ages.
Grapes of Wrath, John Steinbeck	Convinced me that injustice by the powerful was just about the worst of human sins and that nature is not as cruel as we are.
"Life," E. B. White	An article that beautifully captures the whole of life in a paragraph.
The Lives of a Cell: Notes of a Biology Watcher, Lewis Thomas	Made a lot of sense regarding the wisdom of biology—and that it's okay to be just a mass of cells.
Everest: The West Ridge, Thomas Hornbein	Taught me that we humans have no limits; smart and dumb, good and bad.
The Temple of the Golden Pavilion, Yukio Mishima	This one taught me that any evil will seem reasonable to the one committing the evil.

~ Music ~

My friend Tricia's car used to display this bumper sticker: *Life without music would be a mistake*. I agree. Music finds internal places I didn't know existed, it sharpens my feelings and helps me express what I sometimes don't know how else to express. Those listed are not the most impressive, but those that spoke to me and helped ensure my life is not a mistake.

Joan Baez	Bob Dylan	Judy Collins
The Brothers Four	Chuck Berry	Janis Joplin
Jimmy Rogers	Elvis Presley	The Beach Boys
Dave Brubeck	Tom Waits	Peter, Paul and Mary
Willie Nelson	Elton John	Simon and Garfunkel
We Five	Fleetwood Mac	B.B. King
Muddy Waters	The Rolling Stones	Sarah Brightman
Neil Diamond	Lead Belly	Johnny Cash

~ Movies and Plays ~

I experience most movies in layers. I rarely attend a movie theater Instead, my wife and I watch at home, usually chatting as we watch. It takes three or four viewings before we actually see the entire movie. This slow-building understanding encourages watching a given movie multiple times, each time giving us greater awareness of the plot, characters and the skill of the moviemakers, as well as a greater understanding and appreciation of the movie's message.

Groundhog Day

I love the idea that if we're smart, we can make good use of time. I could learn the piano!

In the Heat of the Night

There is societal stuff and personal stuff; both are equally significant—for what is one without the other?

Sophie's Choice

A microcosm of all I hate in humanity (saw it once, never again).

The Longest Day

If you have to go to war, have the courage and determination to win it for God and country; but only if you're on the side of right.

Seven Brides for Seven Brothers	Helped me identify my role image: strong and good-looking, able to sweep ladies off their feet, and able to run a farm. It also had a lot to say about the joy of being alive.
Steambath	A play in which God is a Puerto Rican bathhouse attendant.
Fiddler on the Roof	More on the indomitable human spirit.
The Knack and How to Get it	The absurd lifts my spirits.
Death of a Salesman	I'm not sure who I identify with.
Oklahoma	We performed this musical in fifth grade and I learned how fun life could be.
All That Jazz	Living life to the absolute fullest, if not all that well.
The Remains of the Day	Protocol over passion, role over romance, and legacy over life; what a waste.

~ Art and Poetry ~

L ike movies, art and poetry foster a deeper look at what life is about. Life is art and art is life only when a person acts as a lens. Art and poetry can capture a moment, often just the common, everyday activities that make up our lives. I like to think of my life as a form of art. Why not make our lives beautiful in the ways we can?

The Starry Night, Vincent van Gogh	Gave me permission to see the world through my own eyes—and it's a beautiful world.
Christina's World, Andrew Wyeth	Suggests we are alone, and at the same time that we belong somewhere and that we will reach that place.
Nighthawks, Edward Hopper	Portrays my poetic ideal of life—sad, a bit lonely, with joy within reach.
The Great Wave off Kanagawa, Katsushika Hokusai	The world is a big place and we can flounder within sight of a safe haven or a grand ideal.

The Fog Warning, Winslow Homer	The going may be tough, but strength and character will lead to success.
Winged Victory of Samothrace	Helps me feel connected to the ancient times.
David, Michelangelo	Perhaps the most beautiful object I have ever seen. Makes me proud to be human.
"Charge of the Light Brigade," Alfred, Lord Tennyson	Incompetents can be in power; fear them with your lives. Another lesson about finding your own way.
These poems by an unknown Asian noblewoman. When her husband died:	All things that seem Are one dreamer's dream I sleep, I wake How big the bed with none beside
And when her son died:	Now where may he wander That brave hunter of dragonflies
Basho	Listen! a frog Leaping into the stillness Of an ancient pond

And this final portion of a poem by Cees Nooteboon entitled "Basho." For me, the last few lines is how to accept the loss of loved ones—including ourselves:

...See by the water-
side the track of the
poet
on his way to the
innermost snowland,
See how the water
erases it
how the man with the
hat inscribes it again
preserves water and
footprint, capturing
the movement that
has passed,
so that what vanished
is still there as
something that
vanished.

~ Last Words ~

Three options exist for all of us. Easiest is to assume that life has no meaning; we are born, we live and we die. For this group, the idea is to do as well as you can to get through life with as little distress as possible and/or as much pleasure as possible. Selfishness is a defensible morality. Cooperation and competition will be fluid. Your only obligation to life is a biological one, to create progeny. A kid or two and you are through. Or for those with a smidgen of eco-social conscience, add one and you're done. Life is straightforward although not easy.

The second option is to actively believe in one or more of the current higher powers. This is the best way if you are able to do it. It gives you clear direction, security, support, companions and an afterlife, among other considerable benefits. For this group, if we assume we are worshiping the right deity, there are only two concerns. Concern number one is living well enough for acceptance into the afterlife. The second concern is ensuring that your behavior reflects the actual pronouncements of the higher power rather than the less than divine interpretations of self-serving disciples. I imagine that this second challenge would be the more difficult one. How is a person to know the difference?

My advice is to ask yourself, "Would a reasonable God ask me to do such a thing?" Personally, I don't think any credible God would ask anyone to hurt anyone else. Would God create individuals and groups to play the role of spiritual victims for some chosen people? Would a credible God demand unthinking obedience or would a divine personage prefer someone to think critically, then commit wholeheartedly? Mindless or freely devoted? What makes sense? What has value? This kind of questioning, I believe, would be blasphemy to some believers, yet it seems to honor God to question and then believe. How valid can anything be that discourages scrutiny?

The third option is the one I chose: life has meaning only if you make it so. Giving up God, on an intellectual level, was about the same as giving up Santa Claus. I loved the idea of an immortal being keeping track of who is naughty or nice and giving wonderful gifts to those He favored. Just the possibility of such benevolence made me happy. Over time, however, and sadly, I accepted my truth.

My option means having to create meaning. Meaning to me is to express myself, contribute the best I can and also do my best not to interfere with others living their lives as well as they can. The big, the grand, the powerful, the historic, the divine blind us to our actual independent choices and responsibilities. The meaning of life is not monumental. You can contribute by cleaning up after yourself in the break room. Uncertainty about what is meaningful should be expected; keep seeking ways to contribute as you learn what you need to know. I believe each of us can discover how to become fulfilled within our perspective of what life is and our chosen role in the evolution of the universe.

I must contribute by supporting other people's worthiness and by adding value to the world and my own personal universe however I can. Just living life is not enough.

Did I find the essence of life I was seeking? Maybe. I know what I want out of life and I know what the meaning of life is, I'm still not sure what the essence of life is. I think it is paying attention to the moment, but also allowing the mind to drift in spontaneous ways. I think it is belonging to a larger entity and also being selfish. I think it is in receiving a lot and giving more. Simply put, the essence of life is to value your own and all other life. Yet I still seek a better understanding. That's the best I can do and, I think, all that needs to be done.

When I can no longer meaningfully contribute to the greater community, I hope I can spend my time enjoying the life around me when I wake up in the morning. There are books to read, music to hear, sights to see and people to love. Then, when it's time, my intention is to take a death-with-dignity pill like my friend Malcolm. If that is impossible for some reason, I have a plan B.

When I can no longer contribute, thrive or grow, it's the ice floe for me. And—that's it. My turn will be over.

~ Book Club Questions ~

1. Can people have different meanings of life through their lives?

2. Can different people have different meanings? Should they?

3. Can people live moral lives without believing in God?

4. Should meaning be an individual discovery or found in the wisdom of our ancestors?

5. Is there a difference in "meaning in life" and "meaning of life?"

6. Is it necessary to have meaning?

7. How would you define "a good life?"

8. Can "love" be the meaning of life?

9. What are your thoughts about "death with dignity?"

10. How involved is God in our lives?

~ Acknowledgments ~

My friend Richard Hayenga was the first to read a complete draft. He came over to discuss his reactions late one morning over coffee on our back deck. We discussed his ideas into the early evening over Scotch.

After reading a draft, my brother-in-law Danny Williams provided a number of editorial suggestions, all of which I added. Later, over lunch, he also offered these words of wisdom: "Just because you really like something is no reason to add extra to your sandwich."

David Antrobus was my editor and was recommended by someone I respect. He has a light touch and a sharp eye. I recommend him without reservation although any errors in this work are all David's fault.

D. E. Kissman was kind enough to offer to be a beta reader. It was useful to have someone who didn't know me take a look at an early version.

Jim Minard was also a beta reader, one with an extensive background in philosophy and psychology. It was if Freud, Adler, Jung and the Buddha all took a look.

I must always thank Deena Brown, my wife. With every book she puts up with a distracted husband who bolts out of bed in the middle of the night to capture a great idea, making a lot of noise, and waking her and the two cats. The book is a constant in the front of my mind for months. In fact, she puts up with me focusing on writing at the most unforgivable of times. Luckily, she's not the kind to be compiling a payback checklist.

More about the Author

Robert Brown began serious writing in junior high school when he coedited an underground newspaper called "The Daily Censored," out every other week or so with the motto, "All the news that fits, we print."

He has written numerous articles and more than a dozen books on golf, business management, living life to the fullest and three novels.

Bob lives with his wife and a few animals, wild and domestic, in the Seattle area.

Personal Wisdom

Making Sense of You Others and the Meaning of Life

Robert Brown
Author of Things I Learned From My Wife

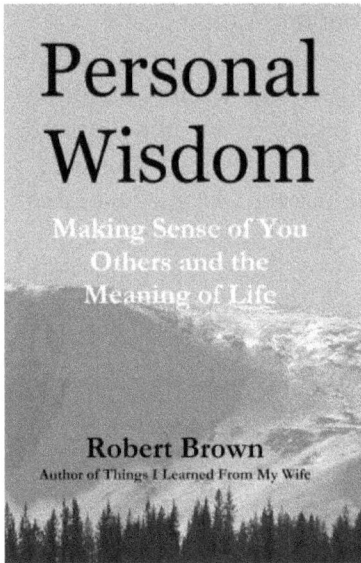

Bob's ideas, tips and tools to live an absolutely wonderful life.

Bob learned early and often that a wife has wisdom beyond male understanding.

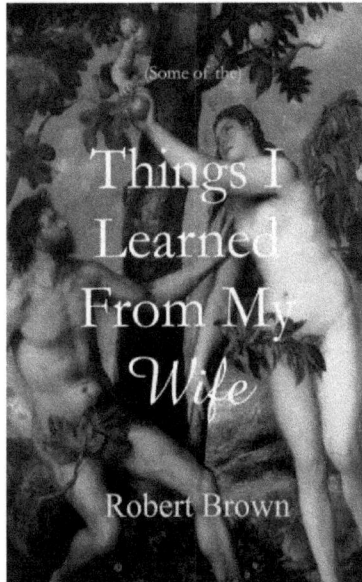

(Some of the)

Things I Learned From My Wife

Robert Brown

The story of a DNA researcher who keeps a promise by experimenting on himself.

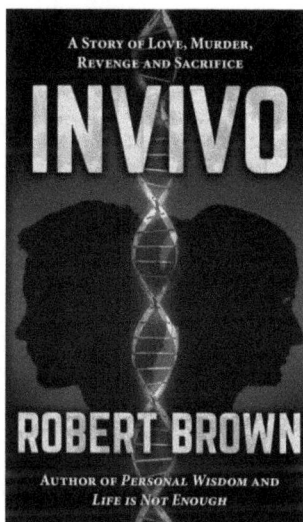

A STORY OF LOVE, MURDER, REVENGE AND SACRIFICE

IN VIVO

ROBERT BROWN

AUTHOR OF *PERSONAL WISDOM* AND *LIFE IS NOT ENOUGH*